# WARFARE WEAPONS

## 13 WEAPONS AND ONE SUPERWEAPON

# Warfare Weapons

## "MIGHTY THROUGH GOD"

SPIRITUAL
ARMAMENT
FOR WINNING
LIFE'S BATTLES

# K. NEILL FOSTER

Christian Publications
Camp Hill, Pennsylvania

Horizon Books
3825 Hartzdale Drive
Camp Hill, PA 17011

*Faithful, biblical publishing since 1883*

ISBN: 0-88965-114-0
LOC Catalog Card Number: 95-75496
© 1995 by Horizon Books
All rights reserved
Printed in the United States of America

95 96 97 98 99   5  4  3  2  1

*Warfare Weapons* is a revised edition of a book previously
published under the title *The Happen Stance*.

# Contents

# Preface to the 1995 Edition

*My friends tell* me that this is the most helpful book I have ever written. Perhaps they are correct. There is a background to this text that deserves mention. It was written shortly after a tremendous spiritual battle. It is now commonly called (and known as) spiritual warfare.

The incident involved a lengthy case of demonization. The struggle went on for seven months before victory came. My exposure to the warfare extended for six weeks. It was a day and night battle. The prisoner was a seventeen-year-old girl who had given way to a legion of the evil powers.

The violence early on was considerable. It took five men to subdue a slender girl. The New Testament came alive as we witnessed reenactments of those things about which we had only read.

The year was 1963. The occasion for the bondage was backsliding on the point of baptism followed by the use of LSD before it had ever become well known. There were demons from the Hungarian war, demons which enabled the victim to perform exquisite Thai dances though she had never been in the Orient. But I spare you.

This text was written before spiritual warfare came into vogue, before evangelical sensibilities (and editors) would allow blow-by-blow descriptions of warfare events.

Essentially, I have enumerated what I discovered were the "weapons of our warfare." If you read between the lines, you will benefit immeasurably more since these insights about warfare weapons were learned in the heat of battle.

This volume was published earlier with Thomas Nelson under the title *The Happen Stance*. But the title died before its time, hindered by its inexactness and my failure to really explain what the book was all about.

Those problems are faced this time. This is a book about spiritual warfare. These are the weapons of warfare as I understood them after a six-week intensive study one can never get in any seminary. *Warfare Weapons* needs to be read for what it actually says, but also for what it implies, for what is certainly there "between the lines." The battle had not long subsided when these lines were written. Thirty years and more of ministry have followed. There have been many like battles in our ministry since, but none so dramatic nor educational as the first.

Welcome to the arsenal!

K. Neill Foster, Ph. D.
Camp Hill, Pennsylvania
November, 1994

# INTRODUCTION

*THE TENT WAS* rippling in the breeze. The crowd was not especially large that August morning on the prairies of Saskatchewan, but our speaker had given a great message. The silence of the people said a whole lot about what they felt.

They had sensed the unction of the Holy Spirit upon the servant and the service. The message had been Christ-honoring and devil-defeating because the minister had taken for his subject "Binding Satan."

"Victory is ours through Christ," he had said. "Isn't it time we sent in the offensive team?" His hour-long theme had been "the authority of the Christian believer." Now finished with his message, he closed in prayer.

But he was not through!

As he stepped off the platform onto the grass floor of the tent, he shouted one word loud and clear—"CHARGE!"

It was electrifying. And in the Spirit. It was not long before I began to toy with that word. "CHARGE! CHARGE!" I liked it. It seemed to say something I had been thinking for a long time.

I had been in Christian warfare at various times

throughout the years. I had even developed a series of Bible studies on "The Weapons of Our Warfare." But the circulation had been only 2,000 copies. The only publisher who had seen the material had rejected it. And deep within I had agreed with him.

Somehow that whole area of truth had to be popularized. Nothing had to be changed, but somehow I had to put flesh on those old bones. Somehow I had to find a way to express the excitement that comes when one really knows the Lord Jesus Christ as the conquering Lion of Judah. This volume is my attempt to put flesh on those bones.

# CHAPTER 1

---

## THE FOUNDATION:

# THE PERSON OF JESUS CHRIST

*BEFORE WE LAUNCH* fully into this discussion of Christianity on the offensive, we must observe that each of our spiritual weapons is vitally related to the person of Jesus Christ. This relationship is not contrived. The foundation for each chapter that follows is that it must finally focus on the Lord Jesus Christ. He is our victory. And so we are taking fourteen different ways to arrive at the same person—Jesus, the Lord.

I have determined that every chapter must lift up Jesus Christ. And so in the pages that follow He is declared—as He was in New Testament times. If it were not such a weary cliché, I would close every chapter with the words, "Christ is the answer."

But cliché or not, it is a fact. And I say it carefully. I know of no human problem, difficulty, or trial which cannot find resolution in Christ: a broken marriage; a broken heart; wayward children; financial reverses; sorrow and bereavement; sinfulness; defeat; depression; discouragement; sickness; obnoxious personality traits; deteriorating cultures; nations under impending judgment. For all of these problems—and many more—Jesus Christ is the answer.

Why is Christ the answer?

Because He is the Word.
Because He is the object of our praise.
Because we pray through Him.
Because we pray in His mighty name.
Because His blood still avails.
Because all authority is given to Him.
Because He is the Savior who fasted.
Because He is one with the Father in perfect unity.
Because He is the one whom we confess.
Because He is the author and finisher of our faith.
Because He surrendered unconditionally to the Father.
Because He suffered for our sins.
Because the gifts of the Holy Spirit are expressions of His body.
Because He is love personified.
Because He is God.

After his resurrection Jesus Christ ascended into heaven. He now sits at the right hand of the

Father, far above all spiritual darkness. Jesus reigns now through His children in this world. His purposes are being fulfilled. World events are controlled by our Lord now. And as the world lurches toward Armageddon, apparently out of control, divine purposes are nevertheless being fulfilled.

Another day is coming. Christ will return to this earth. He will openly seize the reins of human government and usher in the golden age. This is reason enough, I say, to shout encouragement in the battles here and now.

So take courage!

Fight on!

Press your battle!

Charge—in Jesus' name!

## Fire

Fire consumes. It begins with a tiny flicker or a wisp of smoke. But fire in full bloom is a roaring, devouring, destroying force.

God's Word is like a fire and we do well never to forget it. Korea currently is a country where Christianity is on the march. On at least two occasions, crowds numbering more than one million persons have assembled to hear the Christian gospel.

But the Korean flame was introduced by one (mark that, one) convert who led nearly his whole village to Christ even before the arrival of the first Protestant missionary, Horace Allen. A hundred years later the converts number in the millions. The present goal in South Korea is to have a Bible-teaching church within walking distance of every Korean.

We do not play with fire. Only children or fools do that. But we must never forget that God's Word in our hands is "like a fire."

In every nation, the men and women of real influence are not the politicians, the presidents, or the prime ministers. They are those who spread the fire. History hinges upon the Church of Jesus Christ.

## Deliverance

The delivering power of God's Word is also remarkable. Jesus Christ cast out the spirits "with his word" (Matthew 8:16). The demons today are still driven out by the Scriptures. The Word of God, plainly read or preached, is powerful enough to effect deliverance from occult subjection and satanic bondage. If the devil could tear pages out of the Bible, he would certainly tear out those pages that describe Christ's authority, the victory of Calvary, and the mastery believers have under Christ's authority over his evil kingdom.

Paul declared the Word of God was not bound (2 Timothy 2:9). And John believed the young men were strong because "the word of God abideth in you, and ye have overcome the wicked one" (1 John 2:14).

God's Word does overcome. Yet many times we preach, print or share the Word of God without realizing its overcoming power.

Against the kingdom of darkness, the Word is lethal, explosive, deadly. It can blast away human notions and satanic delusions.

## *Hunting Moose*

I am not a great hunter (my wife would surely agree), but I love to hunt the northern moose. Twenty minutes from my door in Alberta, Canada is the wilderness. On my first moose hunt, about half an hour after we arrived in the hunting area, a bull came toward me through the trees. He was so close I could not see him through the scope on my borrowed .308 caliber rifle. I shot and he bolted sideways, but did not fall. Later one of my companions made the kill.

The next day as my partner and I were walking along, crossing frozen beaver ponds, there was the sound of crashing animals in the bush. Moments later a cow moose and her calf moved into plain view and paused to gaze at their intruders.

We fired our rifles and the animals tumbled. It was a rich reward. The surging feelings within seemed to be primordial. Perhaps there is a hunter buried deep in every man.

Later, I had a feeling of awe for the rifles and bullets. The results had been so decisive and final. I am sure, if we only knew it, if we only could see the invisible, the Word of God is a mighty, mighty weapon. God help us to aim it well.

## *Sword Work*

The Bible is often likened to a sword. "Take . . . the sword of the Spirit, which is the word of God" (Ephesians 6:17), said Paul. The writer to the

Hebrews said, "For the word of God is quick, and powerful, and sharper than any twoedged sword, piercing even to the dividing asunder of soul and spirit, and of the joints and marrow, and is a discerner of the thoughts and intents of the heart" (Hebrews 4:12).

A sword cuts, pierces, rips apart. It kills and destroys. It conquers. It is an offensive weapon which is greatly feared. Before the advent of guns, it was the key to success or failure in war.

But I don't want you to think of only the Bible as God's Word. Focus on Jesus, the Son. In the first chapter of John's Gospel, He is the Son of God, eternal, divine, incarnate, the living Word. John sees Him ultimately as the Word who shall reign forever (Revelation 19:13).

So often we have quoted Hebrews 4:12 and almost invariably we have taken it to refer to the written Word of God.

But what fascinates me is the verse that follows. The writer has been talking about the Word of God, about the sword. Now he immediately says, "Neither is there any creature that is not manifest in *his* sight, but all things are naked and opened unto the eyes of *him* with whom we have to do" (4:13, italics mine). Clearly, the writer is speaking of a Person.

Jesus Christ is the Word. He is the Sword of the Spirit. He pierces and divides.

Jesus is the Word. Conquer your circumstances through the Word!

## CHAPTER 2

---

### WEAPON #1:

# THE WORD

*GO FLY A* kite!

Jump in the lake!

Drop dead!

These are phrases common to our North American culture. Supposedly, they are meaningless. In fact, they are the careless expressions of people who have somehow lost the full meaning and impact of words.

But in Africa, for example, one does not say such things lightly. The words might be interpreted as curses, with all the unpleasant associations a curse implies.

We may smile at the strange superstitions of the Africans. After all, words are just words. But are they? Even in North America there is no real happiness found in the home where husband and wife curse each other.

And every war in history started with words.

Yes, deeds were involved, but so were words.

The most influential men in history are not those who warred or built. They are those who philosophized. They are those who founded religions or wrote books. They are those who used words.

Personally, I believe the Christian's Bible is cross-cultural. What it says is true in Boston or Bombay. But in its teachings about words, the Scriptures will be more easily understood in those cultures where words have not yet lost their meaning.

The Bible makes a strong case for the power of men's words. King Saul, rascal that he was, feared Samuel's words (1 Samuel 28:20). Later in Israel's history, the people "rested" on the words of their king (2 Chronicles 32:8). In the case of the patriarch Job, his "comforters" were breaking him into pieces with their words (Job 19:2).

Jesus taught, "For by thy words thou shalt be justified, and by thy words thou shalt be condemned" (Matthew 12:37). He also said of the believing person, ". . . he shall have whatsoever he saith" (Mark 11:23).

And if human words are endowed with such great possibility, how much more power do the words of God Almighty have!

## Tidy Creation

First, God's words have creating power. God did not build this universe by piling one galaxy upon another. He simply said, "Let there be light" (Genesis 1:3)—and there was light. Speech was enough. This beautiful world, this fabulous world, came into being when God spoke.

As a sidelight, it is interesting to note that evolution today is being destroyed by scientists themselves. And scientific creationism is having a field day because so many things being discovered today corroborate the book of Genesis. God spoke and it was so. For a tidy creation you can't beat the spoken word!

## Words That Rip

God's words also convict (Ezra 9:4). Many ministers have no doubt had similar experiences, but there have been times when the Word of God has seemed like a sword in my hand. I recall an occasion in a church in Ontario when God's Word seemed to have such power that every hearer was absolutely still. Every foot seemed riveted to the floor. And the silence was overwhelming. Such is the convicting power of God's Word.

There have been other times, however, when the words I have preached seemed like chaff. Sometimes the problem has been my failure to buttress every statement with God's Word. Illustrations alone are powerless. But when apt illustrations are based upon biblical truth, they rip right into the heart.

One of the many beautiful functions of the Holy Spirit is to cleanse Christ's Church by the "washing of water by the word" (Ephesians 5:26).

He cleanses our Lord's Church with the Word of God. No sincere Christian can honestly and openly read the Bible without experiencing this cleansing. The Bible is like a high-pressure hose directed against a gravel bank. The sand and stones are swept away. One of the reasons Bible camps and conventions are so blessed of God is that the people present are deeply cleansed by the Word.

So too, those who come to Christ for the first time often experience such cleansing that they say, "I feel so clean now!" Such is God's forgiveness. "If we confess our sins, he is faithful and just to forgive us our sins and to cleanse us from all unrighteousness" (1 John 1:9).

## *Healing Too*

God's words also have healing power. "He sent his word, and healed them . . ." (Psalm 107:20). It certainly must be admitted that an emphasis on Christian healing has not always been Christ-adorning. It is true many charlatans and immature brethren have carried forth all kinds of antics and erratic behavior under the name of Christian healing. It is also true Jesus warned that false prophets would come in His name and perform miracles and manifest all kinds of charismatic abilities.

Despite the deceptions, however, God does heal the sick through His Word. And in every church (at least nearly every church which faithfully teaches the Bible) there are those who will testify of healing. They are credible people, unaccustomed to lying and deception and they say, "I have been healed by Jesus Christ." I personally have heard enough such testimonies to convince me that people today still experience divine healing.

Sometimes the healings occur as people sit under the preaching of the Word of God. In an atmosphere of faith, an anointed message on physical healing from the Word of God is likely to produce healings in the congregation, prior to and apart from the laying on of hands (Mark 16:18) or the anointing with oil (James 5:14).

I well remember hearing the late V. Raymond Edman of Wheaton, Illinois, preach about divine healing in Vancouver, British Columbia. There were healings in the crowd as he spoke, I recall, and no one seemed surprised.

No better therapy can be prescribed for the sick than the consistent reading of the Bible. It is itself healing power.

God's Word melts the ice (Psalm 147:18) and surely it melts icy hearts as well. Those who preach God's Word with spiritual power have often seen its effect upon people. First, there is rapt attention, then glistening eyes, and many times the flow of tears. What other centuries-old book can produce such an effect?

## Change Plus

Habits, life-styles and thought patterns are all changed by the same melting Word whether preached or shared, whether to crowds or just one-to-one. God's Word melts hearts.

It also has consuming and breaking power. It is like a hammer and like a fire (Jeremiah 23:29). One can pound a rock with a sledgehammer for a long, long time without apparent result. But the moment comes. The rock at last must crack and splinter.

I believe many who bring the Word of God against seemingly impossible objects do not realize just how powerful God's Word is. Too many times they stop hammering just when the rock of circumstances is about to crumble before them!

## CHAPTER 3

---

### WEAPON #2:

# PREVAILING PRAYER

*THERE'S A COUNTRY* gospel song that says, "Turn your radio on." It means "Tune in to God for prayer." Some might doubt that any valuable spiritual truth could ever come through a song that the "gittar pickers" love. But this time they are wrong. A powerful—and profound—spiritual truth is entwined in that twangy tune!

The fact that man can speak to Almighty God through prayer and with his request move the hand of Omnipotence has to be important and exciting. How well I recall having to leave home for an extended preaching tour when our little girl was just sixteen days old. She had already wrapped her tiny fingers around her daddy's heart.

I wasn't very far into the preaching tour before I began to think about the return trip. I was to finish the tour in New Brunswick before returning to my home in British Columbia. It would take me four long days on the train to reach home.

So while I was still in Ontario, an itinerant evangelist still dependent upon freewill offerings, I prayed something like this: "Lord, if You will bring in $___ in this church (I specified the dollar amount. It was more than I had ever received as an evangelist anywhere.), I will know it is Your will for me to fly home when the tour is over."

When the church presented its offering, it was larger than any I had ever received, even larger than the amount for which I had been praying. I reserved my plane ticket for the Monday following the conclusion of my ministry in Saint John, New Brunswick.

Before I began my closing series in Saint John, I prayed about the amount of the offering there, too. However, when it was presented it was $61 short of the amount for which I had prayed.

Then I wondered. Should I take the long train ride after all? Or should I fly as planned? The decision wasn't hard because I wanted very much to get home!

Early that June morning in 1964 I flew out of Saint John, New Brunswick. The Atlantic glistened beneath me. Montreal. Toronto. Then to Vancouver and the Pacific Ocean, all in the same day. I caught the early afternoon flight to Kamloops—and to my waiting family. My wife and son and our baby were there to meet me; it was great to be home.

My wife then said, "Guess what!—The doctor returned one-half of the fee paid when Donna was born." The fee had been $125. The figures spun through my mind. One half of $125 is $62.50. I was $61 short on my tour. "Oh, Praise the Lord!"

Believe me, in the days after that event, anyone who got near me was likely to hear my story of an exciting answer to prayer!

God really does answer prayer and it is absolutely exhilarating to catch His thought, pray it back to Him and then see the answer.

The Scriptures say a great deal about prayer and whole libraries could be written about it. So it is difficult to say something in one chapter that will be both adequate and helpful, but I will try.

## Desperation Prayers

First, there are desperation prayers. In Exodus 32:32 Moses' prayer is recorded. In great agony he asked God to forgive the people or blot his name out of His book. Jehovah answered. Though Israel was punished, she was forgiven.

I believe today God still responds to desperation prayers. There have been a few times through the years when God has given me this kind of prayer. I suppose some people would call it "intercessory" prayer. But when God gives this kind of prayer to His children, the results are very often miraculous and explosive.

In 1968, after a year in Texas studying Spanish and another year in Puerto Rico stabilizing ourselves in the language, we returned to Alberta. We wanted to settle in Beaverlodge, but no houses seemed to be available. We went to our summer convention still not knowing where we would live in the fall.

Then we received news of an accident. Mr. and Mrs. Chris Sylvester, friends of my parents for many years, had been instantly killed in a train-camper accident.

Sometime later another fact dawned. Their house in Beaverlodge, with all its furniture, was available. Not wishing to appear indecently in haste and yet needing a house very much, we approached the family. I bought the house from the estate *even though my wife disagreed.*

Then I left for some special meetings and the trouble began. The devil jumped on my back and said, "You have made a mistake. You are out of God's will. Something will happen to your family. You have the wrong house. You are not saved." Never had I faced such an assault from the enemy.

I canceled the deal. Then I changed my mind again. And again. And again. It was terrible. Finally, my pastor, Rev. Ches House phoned. "Neill, you have got to stop vacillating." (Part of the uncertainty, I am sure, was the lack of agreement between my wife and me.)

Victory came when Pastor Keith Salway and I went to his little church at Alberta Beach. We prayed throughout a whole afternoon. It was desperation prayer. But the satanic assault was broken. I was freed from oppression.

That house became ours and we enjoyed it very much. It became ours through desperation prayer.

## *Jehovah-Rapha*

Prayer for healing is another fact of this beautiful weapon God has given His children. Early in the Scriptures, Abraham prayed for the healing of Abimelech's household. Later, Jehovah's name is revealed: Jehovah-Rapha—"I am the Lord that healeth thee" (Exodus 15:26).

It is God's nature to heal the sick. The apostles and our Lord Himself prayed for the sick. James made clear, "The prayer of faith shall save the sick" (James 5:15).

For a long time I could not dare to believe God wanted to heal people. In Bible college days I was required to preach a sermon on divine healing and I produced a masterpiece of evasion. No modernist or liberal could have done any better.

Then, as my ministry later unfolded, I began *to dare to begin to hope to believe* that God wanted to heal people. And healings began to take place.

But not everyone was healed and I would be lying to say I wasn't disturbed.

Later, a pastor friend of mine helped me very much. He said, "It is God's highest will to heal." His statement became my personal conviction, and is basic to this day to my faith when I am asked to pray for the healing of others. Healings will not take place if we are equivocating. If we always preface our prayers with "If it be Thy will . . . ," nothing will happen.

At the same time, God permits sickness and suffering and He uses these too. There seems to me to be a happy middle ground which allows a Christian to joyfully pray for healing and to believe that God really delights to heal, while at the same time recognizing that suffering can and does come.

Often, the secret of praying for healing is to catch God's thought and pray it back again.

When I was a young pastor, a lady came to me, showed me her eczema-covered hands, and asked for prayer. Since the following day was Sunday and Communion was to be served with the elders of the church present, I gave her a book to read and suggested she respond the next day when prayer was to be offered.

She did. And the elders and I anointed her with oil and prayed according to what the Bible says in James chapter five. When opportunity to testify was given, she stood and rather excitedly waved her hands before the people. "Look at my hands! Look at my hands!" she exuded.

Unconverted young people from the choir crowded around to see what had happened. Her hands had been perfectly cleansed. The next day she showed them to me. They were covered with clean new skin like that of a baby.

One saintly little lady, weighing only ninety pounds or so but a real heavyweight in the prayer ring, told me the next day, "You know, I couldn't sleep all last night. I have never seen anything like that."

Neither had I. But I am sure prayer in God's will was the key.

## Assassination by Prayer?

Another kind of prayer can be directed against evil men. Isaiah sent word to King Hezekiah that God had heard the prayer he had prayed against Sennacherib, King of Assyria.

Subsequently, 185,000 Assyrians were slain, and later still Sennacherib was assassinated by his own sons. I believe there may be times in our lives when, through prayer, we may find it necessary to wage holy war on wicked men. National and international events can be influenced by prayer. I am not, of course, suggesting we pray for assassinations, but men can rise and fall in other ways. Christians have a potential for spiritual event control through prayer. It is the "happenstance."

Salvador Allende was the Marxist president of Chile. When I visited that country just a few weeks after the military coup had overturned his regime, I discovered that many believers felt Chile had been saved by an act of God. In one church, the young people had been praying for a year for national deliverance. A Communist bloodbath had been stopped in the nick of time.

Now I am not necessarily suggesting that Christians organize a "pray-against campaign" to unseat wicked rulers and politicians. But the time may come when such steps are necessary. At the same time, if Christians can catch God's thoughts in such a matter, they may discover that God wants to influence national and international events through them.

(For some fascinating sidelights of World War II, the story of Rees Howells and his prayers is recommended reading.[1])

## Don't Pray?

Another illuminating thing about prayer is that sometimes it is the wrong thing to do. On three occasions the Lord told Jeremiah *not* to pray for the people (Jeremiah 7:16, 11:14, 14:11). Evidently, judgment was imminent. In the New Testament, John also talks about a time when prayer is inappropriate (1 John 5:16). Many believe such a no-prayer situation indicates that a line of no return has been passed and prayer is not to be offered.

There may be other situations, too, where prayer is not really what God wants. I think this is especially true in the use of Christian authority in deliverances which I will discuss in later pages. For example, if God wants you to use a spoken command and you pray that the Lord will do the work, you are "mis-praying." God in His grace may deliver the victim anyway. But again, catching God's thought exactly might eliminate the prayer completely and replace it with an authoritative, spoken command.

## Catching God's Thought

I have been suggesting throughout this chapter

that prayer is catching God's thought. Why is this so? First, we have an infirmity in prayer. "Likewise the Spirit also helpeth our infirmities: for we know not what we should pray for as we ought; but the Spirit [himself, NIV] maketh intercession for us with groanings which cannot be uttered. And he that searcheth the hearts knoweth what is the mind of the Spirit, because he maketh intercession for the saints according to the will of God" (Romans 8:26-27).

Paul said, "We know not what we should pray for as we ought." The proof of our problem is that many, many of our prayers are not answered.

In this Romans passage, I see two Intercessors acting on our behalf: first, the Holy Spirit ("The Spirit itself maketh intercession for us") and second, Jesus Christ ("And he that searcheth the hearts knoweth what is the mind of the Spirit").

A.B. Simpson had this to say:

> And so there is a divine and most perfect provision in the economy of grace by which the Holy Spirit adjusts our spirit into such harmony with God that we can catch his thoughts and send it back again, not merely as a human desire but as a divine prayer. True prayer, therefore, is not only the voice of man crying to God but the voice of God in man expressing the deepest needs of the human heart and conveying them to the throne in such a manner that the answer shall be assured.[2]

The heavenly Intercessors combine to reveal to us God's will. Once we know God's will we can pray with confidence. "And this is the confidence that we have in him, that, if we ask any thing according to his will, he heareth us: and if we know that he hear us, whatsoever we ask, we know that we have the petitions that we desired of him" (1 John 5:14-15).

One of God's great men of the past said that the biggest difficulty in getting one's prayers answered is to discover God's will. After that, he believed, it is relatively simple to get the prayer answered.

## Be Wise

So this whole ministry of prayer comes right back to the Holy Spirit and to Jesus Christ. Together they reveal to us the Father's will.

We are not to be unwise, but rather we are to understand the Lord's will. Paul taught that. And he also explained how: through the fullness of the Holy Spirit and through the indwelling fullness of Jesus Christ (see Ephesians 5:17-18).

We have come full circle. Prayer begins with our Lord Jesus Christ in the heart. When He is there He simply says, "If ye shall ask anything in my name, I will do it" (1 John 5:14). Then He puts His thoughts in our hearts.

We pray His heart burdens back to Him! And the excitement begins!

## CHAPTER 4

---

## WEAPON #3:

# PRAISE

*PRAISE TO THE* Lord God is as old as eternity. And it is as enduring as God's future. The Bible is full of such praise, and anything that is that prominent in God's Word has to be important—and powerful. Praise in the Bible is both prominent and powerful.

The biblical books of First and Second Chronicles have significant teaching on praise. For example, when David numbered 38,000 Levites, 4,000 were assigned to praise the Lord (1 Chronicles 23:3-5). That has to be an atrocious use of manpower—unless praise is terribly important. The importance of praise to David is also shown by his appointment of Asaph and others to minister continually before the Lord (1 Chronicles 16:4, 6, 37).

These Scriptures imply to me that not only was the Old Testament tabernacle in all its parts rich in spiritual significance, but the worship itself was rich in continual sound.

Apparently, too, those who praised the Lord were not dependent on an audience. Their responsibility was to praise Jehovah, not to entertain people.

## Sing to Empty Seats

One of our summer convention lecturers related an interesting incident about a church choir in Argentina. At a rehearsal they were challenged by a discerning pastor to praise the Lord without concern for people. They decided to sing to the Lord—and to the empty seats of the church sanctuary. The result, not surprisingly, was a mighty manifestation of God's presence and spiritual renewal.

Rare is the choir these days which would be willing to put on a concert for God alone.

Many Scriptures emphasize praise as a means of access to God. The Levites were appointed to praise in the gates of the tents of the Lord (2 Chronicles 31:2). The psalmist urged, "Enter into his gates with thanksgiving, and into his courts with praise" (Psalm 100:4). And Isaiah declared, "They shall call . . . thy gates praise" (Isaiah 60:18).

I have often thought that there are many things wrong with our Lord's church, but this is one thing that is right. We praise before we preach, we sing before we share. Perhaps it is instinctive. But praise is access. It batters down satanic opposition and it paves the way for the Word of God.

## Shifting the Sword

I have a friend who is an accomplished gospel singer. In the past we did tours together—one night stops and concerts. Our format was interesting because I was perfectly content to allow him to sing for an hour and then I would preach the gospel for ten or fifteen minutes.

Almost invariably the response to the public invitation was gratifying. As far as we were concerned, there was no need to jealously maneuver for equal time because praise and the Word are both powerful weapons. The switch from praising to preaching was no more than the shifting of the Sword of the Lord from one hand to the other.

Praise is also described as a sacrifice, Jeremiah observes that sacrifices of praise were to be brought into the house of the Lord (Jeremiah 33:11). And the writer to the Hebrews urges, "By him [Jesus] therefore, let us offer the sacrifice of praise to God continually, that is, the fruit of our lips giving thanks to his name" (Hebrews 13:15).

## Verbalized Praise

I notice several things about this text in Hebrews. First, the sacrifice of praise is to be the fruit of our lips. I take this to indicate verbalized, spoken praise. I believe one can praise the Lord in his thoughts, but when praise is audible, it seems to convict sinners, cow the devil and waft up to the Lord a cloud of invisible incense and adoration.

I have observed in the Christian experience a phenomenon I call a "spirit of Praise." Sometimes I have felt that way myself. At such times, whenever I have opened my mouth all I have wanted to say was "Praise the Lord!"

I recall, too, meeting a Christian brother in Vancouver, British Columbia. I cannot remember his name or any other details except that when he greeted me, it was with praise to the Lord.

Second, the Hebrews text urges "continual" praise. And life being what it is, a series of hills and hollows, glads and sads, praise is intended by the Lord to be continual in all circumstances. There should never be a time when praise is not on our lips.

And since praise is to be continual, sometimes it is certainly going to be a sacrifice offered with difficulty, without feeling, praise offered only by a sheer act of the will.

With a ministry to conduct, a periodical to publish, and help to pay, I had become very dependent on the mail, perhaps too much so. But it was a trial of faith to pick up a day's mail with only three dollars in it, or perhaps not even a penny, when the bills totaled thousands of dollars. But we have learned to praise the Lord for the three dollars. And we have discovered God takes care of the thousands.

## *Praise God for Evil?*

There are a couple of other Scriptures to be

mentioned here. Paul said, "In *every thing* give
thanks" (1 Thessalonians 5:18, italics mine).
Again, he said, "Giving thanks *always* for *all*
things" (Ephesians 5:20, italics mine). Christian
people cannot obey these commands without offering the sacrifice of praise.

It is apparent that God wants us to praise Him
in all situations. But how can this be? Does God
want us to praise him for evil, for the works of
the devil? Some people think so, but I am not one
of them.

Pastor William F. Bryan of Toledo, Ohio, has
some insights which I wish to include here:

> We are not to praise God for the devil's
> work. When Moses came down from the
> mountains with the tablets of the Law and
> found the children of Israel worshiping a
> golden calf, he did not praise God for their
> unholy orgies. Jeremiah did not praise God
> for the wickedness of his people, and David
> did not praise God for Absalom's rebellion.
> He accepted it as chastening of the Lord
> rather than a cause for praise.
>
> Some of our apostles of praise seem to be
> oblivious to the fact that there is a time to
> live and a time to hate: a time to kill and a
> time to make alive. Their "timing" is so far
> off they would have us praising God for
> drunken fathers, corrupted children, and
> broken homes. We may praise God in all
> things, but we can hardly praise Him for

that which brought suffering and shame. We praise Him for the cross, but not for the sin that made it necessary.[3]

## His Endorsement Necessary

The Ephesians were to give thanks always for all things "in the name of our Lord Jesus Christ." The name of Jesus is a qualifier. It signifies all that He is. Attaching His name to prayer or praise assumes His full nature and character, the endorsement of all that He is.

If a child, for example, has been abducted, abused by a sex maniac, and murdered, shall his Christian parents praise the Lord Jesus Christ for those demonic deeds? Most assuredly not.

But can Almighty God give these distraught parents confidence in the sovereignty of God, the assurance that all things do work together for good for those who love God? Absolutely. Because God's sovereignty, God's ultimate control of all human events, is something to which Jesus Christ can attach His name. These parents could praise God in their trial, even *for* it, but not *for* the demonic acts.

It is easy to praise the Lord for pleasant things, but not for the unpleasant things. Perhaps if we understood praise better, if we realized what it does, we would be more willing to praise God in all situations. Praise is really an assault weapon against Satan. *If evil comes, praise the Lord: not for the evil, but as a declaration of war against it.*

For instance, sometimes thoughts hit me which

I recognize to be straight from the devil's pit. My reaction is "Praise the Lord!" But am I praising the Lord Jesus Christ for those horrid thoughts? Most assuredly not! With praise I go to war and the devil backs off. It is a great remedy. Try it.

So when there is murder, adultery, divorce, bankruptcy, disease, rebellion in the home, praise the Lord. But not for evil. Not for what the devil has done and is doing. But praise the Lord for what *He* is going to do, for what He is, for the good which is going to come out of evil. In the spiritual warfare, praise is an offensive maneuver which triggers all kinds of miracles in the Christian's life.

One of my friends says as a young pastor he was confronted with a medium who went into a trance as he and some others were driving along in a car. Rather carelessly perhaps, he commanded the demons to come out. They promptly did—and attacked him!

Because he was temporarily paralyzed he had to yell to his wife, "Grab the wheel, quick!" Then his godly mother-in-law prayed and he was released.

The spiritist soon went into another trance and when his mother-in-law suggested more prayer, my friend didn't want any part of it. As far as he was concerned, the spiritist could stay in her trance.

But the godly woman persisted, "You are up against a battle and you have got to win it. If you don't, you will be running from the devil all your life."

When he asked her what should be done, her response was unbelievable. "We will sing!" she answered. So they sang, prayed, and "covered" my friend with the blood of Jesus Christ.

Then he again commanded the demons to come out. And though the demonized woman had been tearing at her clothes, frothing at the mouth, and writhing in the back seat of the car, the demons suddenly came out.

Years later, as my friend related this incident publicly, he said, "I learned that day the power of singing."

## Praise Is Logical

Praise is intended to be logical. You do not find a single Psalm which has only "Praise the Lord" as its content. Continually the psalmist urges praise to the Lord—but never vain repetition, never statements of praise without logic locked in. For that reason, we should be careful always to couch our praise to the Lord in rational content. While we are blessing and praising the Lord, one thing we should not be doing is forgetting all His benefits. "Bless the LORD, O my soul, and forget not all his benefits" (Psalm 103:2).

What we are observing here should make us cautious about praise which is devoid of intellectual and logical content. If we are not sure what our praise is all about, we may have to ask ourselves the next question: To whom is this praise directed?

I want to say with kindness, sometimes the praise offered in many very fervent, Bible-believing churches does not go to almighty God or the Lord Jesus Christ at all. Rather, it goes to some unidentified and imprecise Jesus who is not the Lord Jesus Christ.

Biblically, the enactment of praise can come in a number of ways. For instance, it can come through speaking (Psalm 119:171), through singing (Psalm 135:3) and through musical instruments. And when it comes to musical instruments, a long biblical list can be compiled: trumpets, cymbals, harp, psaltery, stringed instruments, timbrels, and wind instruments (2 Chronicles 7:6; Ezra 3:10; 1 Chronicles 25:3; Psalm 43:4; 71:22; 144:9; 149:3; 150:4—The Amplified Old Testament).

## A Physical Act

Praise can be also a physical act. I believe that standing before the Lord with uplifted hands is both an act of praise (Psalm 134) and an act of prayer (1 Timothy 2:8). The significance of upraised hands is often missed. I take it to be a sign of surrender and, at the same time, a sign of victory.

As a young pastor I invited a certain minister to my church. When we prayed together I discovered he raised his hands in prayer. (I couldn't help peeking through my fingers as such a queer fellow!) But his ministry was good, even marvelous, and so I didn't really mind his arm-raising. He also told me some people are so bound spiritually they cannot raise their hands to God.

Not too long after, I was called to a home where a woman wanted to find Christ. She prayed in vain. She was so bound she could not come to Christ. Then I asked her, "Can you lift your hands to the Lord?" No, she could not. Lifting her hands to turn off a light was no problem at all, but to praise the Lord—no way!

Not surprisingly, victory came to her one day when all by herself she finally thrust her hands heavenward. Then it was that God spoke to her and said, "Your sins are forgiven."

Ever since, I have realized the significance of uplifted hands. There are times when I am preaching or dealing with a group of inquirers en masse that I will ask those people to lift their hands to God. Often, too, in my own prayer and praise I will lift my hands to the Lord. It is proper and it is good.

## *Skip the Trip*

Unfortunately, some have made a fetish out of upraised hands. It has become a measure of how much spiritual freedom people have and a trip laid on worshipers who may not be at all led by the Holy Spirit to lift their hands.

Sometimes, it seems to me, one of our most human traits is to twist the good into the extreme. Frankly, I have been downright uncomfortable in the presence of some of the hand-raising I have seen. It may be praise—but to whom?

Praise is proper in many settings: before the Lord (Psalm 9:2), in His sanctuary (Psalm 150:1), in the congregation (Psalm 22:22, 25), and before people and nations (Psalm 57:9).

Before people and nations? Apparently it won't hurt the world of unbelievers to hear the saints praise the Lord!

## *It Has an Edge*

In fact, praise has a finely honed evangelistic edge. It brings people to Christ. Notice, too, that David was going to praise Jehovah "before the gods." We can praise God before the devil and his hosts.

Remember, you are not praising the devil. Rather, you are reciting, even, if I dare say it cautiously, flaunting your faith before Satan. It is a great expression of confidence in the fact that "all things work together for good."

It is fascinating, too, to notice in the world who praised the Lord. Heaven, earth, the seas, and everything that moves therein may praise the Lord (Psalm 69:34). Sun, moon, stars, fire, hail, snow, vapors, stormy wind, mountains, hills, fruitful trees, beasts, creeping things, flying fowl, kings of the earth, all people, princes, judges, young men, maidens, old men, and children may all praise the Lord (Psalm 148). Sailors, isles of the sea, and their inhabitants may praise the Lord (Isaiah 42:10). Finally, the psalmist says, "Let everything that hath breath praise the LORD" (Psalm 150:6).

I even look at a mountain differently now. Many times my wife and I sat at our window for just a few minutes before it was time to go to the office. I had coffee and she had tea. And from her chair when it was clear, she could see the mountains more than a hundred miles away. In the morning a peak we called Teepee Mountain was especially striking—a craggy, snow-covered spire soaring into the horizon. That mountain was and is busy praising God!

And the fruitful trees. They lift their arms toward heaven. Their leaves flutter in the breeze. We may not realize it until the Scriptures lay hold on us, but those millions of leaves and those stately trees are all praising God.

## Even Prince

Perhaps I am naive, but I believe even a dog can praise the Lord. I am a dog lover. And if you care to know, our "Prince" had a spiritual history.

The story began when we as a family began to pray for a dog. Then some renters moved into the basement suite of our home. After the husband made the agreement he said, "By the way, we have a dog." It was fine with us. And when their dog sometimes escaped into the upper part of the house to visit us, we stopped praying for a dog.

When the tenants left, we bought Prince for twenty dollars. Prince was regularly remembered in prayer—that he wouldn't get run over. When he got lost, he was prayed home. Once when

Prince had been gone two or three days, my boy prayed, "Lord, let Prince come home when I call the first time." He called, and the dog burst around the corner of the house. Another time he had been lost for several days. Within an hour our cream-colored pooch was home. Once he was lost in the wilderness. But following a back-seat prayer meeting in our car, we found him.

Now Prince was just a little dog like one sees in a circus. Spitz, they say. But when he sat up, when he was hungry or excited, or even when he was guilty, he was clearly one of God's creatures. He praised the Lord, too, because he was alive and because God made him. As brilliant as man is, he can't even make a mongrel.

So praise is everywhere. This whole book could be filled just developing this thought.

Even the ungodly shall praise the Lord (Psalm 76:10). And Nebuchadnezzar, the ungodly king, praised the God of heaven (Daniel 4:37). The angels, too, praise the Lord (Psalm 148:2). Men shall praise Him (Psalm 107). The saints shall praise the Lord (Psalm 149:5-6). And yes, in the future the twenty-four elders shall praise the Lord (Revelation 5:14).

When one realizes from where and from what praise comes to God, the perspective changes. Satan rules this world and ruins it for his own praise. But the mighty chorus of creation praises the Lord God Almighty! What the devil gets through subterfuge and deception is pitifully small after all.

## *Judah Was Special*

Judah was one of the sons of Jacob, a son to whom Jacob gave a prophetic blessing. According to Jacob's words, Judah was to be praised and was to have victory over his enemies. Judah was also to be a "lion's whelp." Neither would the scepter nor lawgiver ever depart from Judah (Genesis 49:8-10).

Marvelous promises were made to the young man Judah. And some of them have been and will be fulfilled in Jesus Christ, the Lion of the tribe of Judah.

But there is something tremendous which I have not shared with you yet. "Judah" means praise. So it is praise which is to bring victory over the enemy. Jesus Christ is the Lion of praise!

These Old Testament figures tell us much about praise. The way God dealt with the tribe of Judah is an indication of the importance He attaches to praise.

For example, the tribe of Judah was placed *first* on the east side of the camp (Numbers 2:3). Judah was *first*, in the lead when Israel journeyed (Numbers 2:9, 10:14). Judah was *first* in the offering of sacrifice (Numbers 7:12). Judah was *first* to fight the Canaanites (Judges 1:2).

These biblical examples indicate the priority God places on praise. There are many things wrong in the church today, but again I say, here is something that is right! No matter which communion, no matter which country, no matter which administration, praise comes before preaching. Praise to God is first, as it should be. True, the enthusiasm and exuberance of praise varies with the different denominations, but praise is always first. Thank God.

## Judah—a Sanctuary

One of the most beautiful truths about Judah is found in Psalm 114:2: "Judah was his sanctuary." I puzzled over that at first, but then it started to make sense. The Lord actually dwells in the midst of His people's praises! Praise is the sanctuary of the Lord. In the church age praise is God's temple!

A number of years ago I had a young man traveling with me as an associate evangelist. He often led the song service and sometimes preached. And frequently told the people, "Let's praise the Lord. The Bible says, 'The Lord dwells in the midst of the praises of his people.' "

Then one day he tried to find that verse in the Bible. To his chagrin, he discovered there is no verse, "The Lord dwells in the midst of the praises of his people." But undaunted, and rather dangerously, he said, "It is not in the Bible, but I believe it anyway!" Later, though, he was very pleased to read Psalm 22:3, "O Thou that inhabitest the praises of Israel."

God does dwell in His people's praises. Praise is God's sanctuary. Judah was (and is) the sanctuary of the Lord. And that is why when we praise the Lord we so often feel His presence. It is all I can do to refrain from writing praises to God right now. These truths are exhilarating! And they are blessed.

## Praise Power

This chapter could be called, "Praise Power" and not without reason. In the arsenal of the Christian, praise is one of the mightiest weapons God has given us. For example, in Psalm 8:2, David said, "Out of the mouths of babes and sucklings hast thou ordained strength. . . ." Jesus, paraphrasing the same passage, put it this way, "Out of the mouth of babes and sucklings thou has perfected praise" (Matthew 21:16).

So, it seems to me, if we are to accept the commentary of the Holy Spirit (the New Testament application of Old Testament truth), praise is equated with strength. Praise is never weakness. It is magnificent power. It is a wholesome, positive kind of event control. Praise makes things happen.

Praise produces visible effects. "And he hath put a new song in my mouth, even praise to our God: many shall see it, and fear, and shall trust in the LORD" (Psalm 40:3). Praise is observable. It produces the fear of God in people. And it carries them through to trust in God. It is a sharp instrument of evangelism. Good evangelistic services need plenty of praise.

The same though surfaces in Psalm 118:21. Praise is linked to salvation. In the book of Acts, the early believers were "praising God and having favor with all the people." We should not be surprised that the Lord "added to the church daily such as should be saved" (Acts 2:47).

There, too, the lame man walked and leaped. Show me a church where the people have learned to praise the Lord and there will be conversions there. And healings. And many miracles. Praise always triggers momentous events.

Praise also brings mighty manifestations of God's glory—spiritual fire! This is illustrated in both 2 Chronicles 5 and 2 Chronicles 7. The singing of the Levites and the praying of King Solomon precede the visible manifestations of God's fire and glory. And the last verse of the gospel of Luke tells us what preceded Pentecost: "And they were continually in the temple, praising and blessing God. Amen" (24:53). Historically, praise preceded Pentecost. And praise will also precede your personal pentecost—and mine!

## *Deliverance Too*

Apparently, praise also has a relationship to deliverance. Paul and Silas were praising God in prison when the prison doors were opened and their chains fell off (Acts 16:25-26). The lesson is clear. Deliverance comes through praise to God, either your own praise or the praise of another.

In spiritual warfare, praise brings victory. Jericho fell to the trumpets of Joshua (Joshua 6). Judah defeated Israel with a shout (2 Chronicles 13:14-15). Singing defeated Ammon and Moab

(2 Chronicles 20:22). And the psalmist makes it clear, there is ". . . triumph in thy praise" (Psalm 106:47).

## Praise Binds

One of the most marvelous lessons in praise is found in Psalm 149. The high praises of God are to be in the mouths of the Lord's people. Such praises have magnificent results. They are like a two-edged sword in the hands of the saints. They bring vengeance and punishment upon the ungodly. They "bind their kings with chains, and their nobles with fetters of iron" (149:8).

I believe these kings and nobles represent the unseen powers of darkness, and praise binds them. It is a great thought, and it lines up with Jesus' teaching about binding and loosing (Matthew 12:29; 18:18). The psalmist makes it clear, just as Jesus implies, "This honor have all his saints" (149:9). Every believer who will praise the Lord can and will bind the powers of darkness. Christian friend, whenever you go to war against the demonic forces of evil, go praising!

## Edginess Too

I must confess, however, that I get uneasy when praise is simply directed to "Jesus." If the person praising has clearly indicated that the praise is directed to the Lord Jesus Christ, fine. I am all for that! But all too often it is some unspecified "Jesus" that praise is given.

I believe that all the charismatic gifts are for

today, including the utterance gifts. But any utterance that refers only to "Jesus" makes me edgy. I know very well, and you should, too, that there are false utterances which praise a certain "Jesus" who is not the Lord Jesus Christ, the Son of God who came in the flesh and is the Lord of lords. Paul warned that there is "another Jesus" (2 Corinthians 11:4). We must be sure all our praise ascends to the Lord Jesus Christ of the New Testament.

## *Final Focus*

Again we see it. The object of praise is the Lord God Almighty. With each of the mighty weapons, including praise, the focus is finally on the Lord Jesus Christ. He is the Victor and the victory.

I will never forget the first time I heard Handel's *Messiah*. "Blessing and honor, and glory, and power, be unto him that sitteth upon the throne, and unto the Lamb for ever and ever" (Revelation 5:13).

The majestic words and melody will never be erased from my mind and heart. If you know that great music perhaps you can hear it now. And if you don't know it, a delightful discovery is still ahead.

All praise, forever and ever, to the King of glory, the Lord Jesus Christ!

## CHAPTER 5

WEAPON #4:

# THE BLOOD

*WHEN THE BRITISH* empire was in its heyday, every rope in the whole Royal Navy had a crimson strand woven into it. The crimson strand told the world the rope was British.

There is a crimson line that runs all through the Bible, too. In the beginning of Genesis, Abel's offering to God was accepted because it was a meat offering, because blood had been shed. There the blood line was established.

The many references to blood in the Old Testament prepare the discerning believer to understand the significance of the blood of Jesus Christ in the New Testament. When Peter, for example, used the phrase, "sprinkling of the blood of Jesus Christ" (1 Peter 1:2), he was stimulating all kinds of recollection in the minds of the Jewish believers in Christ to whom he was addressing his letter. Blood in their scriptural record (the Old

45

Testament) had a very great significance.

To avoid the judgment of the death angel passing through the Egyptian night, the Hebrew children were required to place blood on the door posts. This took place long before Moses received the law of God upon Mount Sinai, but it established in the minds of God's children the importance of blood.

## Levitical Laws

Later the Levitical laws reinforced the concept of the importance of blood. Animals had to die. In the shedding of their blood, remission of sins was secured. The emphasis on blood (which is extreme, because it is life itself to the one who loses it) persistently implied that sin could never be considered as anything less than a terribly grave offense against a holy God. No Hebrew could witness the massive slaughter of animals without realizing that the blood on the altar had cost the animal its life. No Hebrew could watch the river of blood around the Old Testament tabernacle without realizing that the offenses, the sins which required the shedding of blood for remission, must have been very serious actions indeed. The remedy Jehovah required was in itself a mighty lesson. Nothing less than death could bring forgiveness and life to a sinner.

## Gallons of Blood

I was reared on a farm where occasionally I watched the butchering of a farm animal. Often a rifle was used to kill the animal, but I have seen a sledgehammer used to knock a cow into unconsciousness. Then the butcher's razor-sharp knife was thrust into the throat of the animal. And gallons of blood rushed out. Or so it seemed. One does not easily forget such events. They mark the mind. I suppose that is one of the reasons why God decreed the shedding of so much blood in the Old Testament.

When Paul was referring to Old Testament happenings he said, "Now all these things happened unto them [the Hebrews] for examples: and they are written for our admonition, upon whom the ends of the world are come" (1 Corinthians 10:11). Nowhere is this more true than in the many references to blood in the Old Testament.

## The Coming Lamb

Obviously, it would be possible to fill many books with writings about the shedding of blood as it was observed under the Law. But I wish only to establish in the minds of my readers that the killing of lambs and the flow of blood under the Old Covenant simply anticipated and prefigured the shedding of Christ's blood. He is the "Lamb slain from the foundation of the world" (Revelation 13:8).

The blood of bulls and goats, or even lambs, cannot help us today. For the Christian caught in a web of sins and circumstances, assaulted by Satan, pressed beyond measure, only the blood of Jesus Christ avails. Because of the present power of the blood of Jesus Christ, it is still possible to overcome, to win the fight against the awesome powers of the world, the flesh and the devil.

## Present Power

Julius Caesar once had unrivaled power. At its zenith, no earthly power could surpass it. But today anyone can mock the name of Julius Caesar without consequences. The reason is he has no present power. But the blood of Jesus Christ has present power. If his blood is mocked, there are consequences. Peter wrote, "Ye were not redeemed with corruptible things, as silver and gold, . . . but with the precious blood of Christ" (1 Peter 1:18-19).

The application is clear enough. Silver and gold are corruptible. But Jesus' blood is as red and warm as it ever was. Never has it clotted or coagulated. It is incorruptible. And that is why it has present power.

That power is redemptive. Speaking of the Savior, Paul said, "In whom we have redemption through his blood, even the forgiveness of sins" (Colossians 1:14). When Paul was saying farewell to the Ephesian elders, he reminded them that the church had been "purchased with his [Christ's] own blood" (Acts 20:28). (The context suggests God's blood—a powerful argument that Jesus is God.)

## The Currency of Blood

In my travels to various parts of the world I have used many currencies. In the Republic of

Zaire, for example, at one time, one zaire equaled two American dollars. No longer of course.

In the Dominican Republic one peso equaled one American dollar. But that is no longer necessarily true either. Moreover outside these countries these currencies have little value. They are limited by their own geographical and political contexts. In Canada or the United States I cannot use a zaire or a peso.

In contrast to the zaire and the peso, the United States dollar is negotiable nearly worldwide. It shows signs of weakening and it may be replaced by a world currency some day. But right now, if you want to buy something, the best thing in all the world to have is an American dollar. It has purchasing power—redemptive power in the secular sense.

To purchase living souls, to ransom them from Satan's clutches, only one currency will do: the blood of Jesus Christ.

This same blood also has justifying power. "Much more then, being now justified by his blood, we shall be saved from wrath through him" (Romans 5:9). To be justified, in the language of the layman, means, "God took our sins and put them on Christ and then took Christ's righteousness and gave it to us in exchange."[4] Men may receive a new status and attain a new relationship to God through the blood which splashed on Calvary's knoll nearly two thousand years ago. Incredible, but true.

## Not a "Super Saint"

I have a friend who really loves Christ. Some of his habits leave a bit to be desired and he certainly does not come on as a "super saint." But he loves God, and he should. I get the feeling from talking with him that his life was rough before he came to Jesus. He hasn't told me so, but I get the feeling there are not very many sins he hasn't tried.

The thing that impresses me most, though, is how my friend revels in his new relationship with Christ. I would not want anyone to explore the depths of sin just so he could revel in God's righteousness. But for one who has been that sad route, justification is a fantastic thing. It is really, really great.

Now don't forget: The blood of Jesus Christ— which on a certain day of history at a certain time of day was poured out—sets people free now.

Romans 3:25, speaking of Jesus Christ, adds this, "Whom God hath set forth to be a propitiation through faith in his blood." The editors of the Scofield Bible describe propitiation thus:

> The thought in the Old Testament sacrifices and in the New Testament fulfillment is that Christ completely satisfied the just demands of a holy God for judgment on sin by His death on the cross. God, foreseeing the cross, is declared righteous in forgiving sins in the Old Testament period as well as in justifying sinners under the new covenant (Romans 3:25-26; cp. Exodus

29:33). Propitiation is not placating a vengeful God but, rather, it is satisfying the righteousness of a holy God, thereby making it possible for Him to show mercy righteously.[5]

May we justly and properly receive God's mercy today? Of course. Because the blood has present propitiating power.

## God Has a Right to Be Angry

If a wife has been unfaithful, for example, her husband has a just and proper right to be angry with her. But he can also be merciful and forgiving. That is propitiation. Though we deserve hell and judgment it is now possible for us to receive God's mercy—all through the blood, our present propitiating power.

Christ's blood also has pacifying power. Christ "made peace through the blood of his cross" (Colossians 1:20). He reconciled all things unto Himself, Paul adds, and all this through His blood.

## War Somewhere

If peace must be made, there is war somewhere. If pacification must take place, there is rebellion somewhere. And if you think there is no war in the heavenlies, you are mistaken. If you think there is no rebellion in this world, you are blind.

I believe that Jesus' blood makes peace between the angry rebellion of men and the offended holiness of God. God is the sworn enemy of the guerrillas of sin and evil. But the blood, the present power of the blood of Christ, is sufficient to pacify the just wrath of God against sin. Praise God for this present pacifying power.

The blood of Jesus Christ, shed so long ago, cleanses from sin today. "But if we walk in the light, as he is in the light, we have fellowship one with another, and the blood of Jesus Christ, his Son cleanseth us from all sin" (1 John 1:7). And the tense of the verb "cleanseth" indicates that it is a continual cleansing that takes place. Continual! Can you believe it?

A friend once said, "Forgiveness is better than you think!" If you have asked God to forgive you, you are now perfect in His sight—by the blood. Christ has not only cleansed your past sins by His blood, He has also made provision for cleansing your future sins. And if you are "walking in the light," He constantly cleanses you from sin now. It is all included.

## Confession Necessary

This does not negate for a moment the necessity of confession of sin. But who among us can confess the sins we have committed but do not even know about? The Bible, you should realize, says there are sins of ignorance (Leviticus 5:15). And the psalmist prayed, "Search me, O God, and know my heart: try me and know my thoughts: And *see if there be any wicked way in me*" (Psalm 139:23-24, italics mine). The Laodicean church did not even know its true state (Revelation 3:17).

But thank God for the cleansing of the blood of Christ. This truth, like so many others, has to be held in careful perspective and balance. Rejoice in the continual cleansing of Jesus' blood. And stay open and sensitive in the matter of confession of your sins to God—and sometimes to men. God's continual forgiveness never negates the need for confession or repentance.

## Popping in and Out

But the immature Christian who is continually popping in and out of fellowship, depending on whether or not he has confessed every sin in his life, needs to realize that Jesus' blood continually cleanses. And he needs to realize as well that issues still need to be faced and sin still needs to be confessed.

Christ's death dealt a destructive blow to Satan's kingdom (Hebrews 2:14). Jesus talked about the prince of this world being judged and cast out. The implication is clear—the blood of Jesus Christ has awesome destructive power. Satan was destroyed at Calvary.

His destruction was total and complete though it still awaits actuality. Satan is destroyed. That is certain. But until Satan's sentence is executed, he continues to exercise his weakened power. The satanic taproot has been irrevocably cut. We wait only for the leaves to shrivel and die.

I do not know the number of times I have been involved in Christian warfare, nor do I really care. But one constant among several in the warfare is this—the blood of Jesus Christ will blast the enemy loose. Jesus' blood has present overcoming power. It is for the now, the same now in which people live and struggle with their problems.

Through the blood of Jesus also comes protection. Just as the blood upon the doorposts protected Israel as the death angel passed by, so today the blood of Jesus Christ protects and covers.

A while ago my son Jeff was being troubled by nightmares and bad dreams. We felt their source was certainly not divine and so we prayed and placed him "under Jesus' blood." He sensed the difference, though he was just a lad, and he himself began to pray, "Lord Jesus, cover me with Your precious blood."

I believe what you ask for you will receive. If you claim the protective, covering blood of Jesus Christ, you are covered. Probably the only time this is not true is when a person deliberately marches off the safety of biblical ground.

On one occasion I was asked to tape two television programs and give a church address, all on the subject of exorcism. Instinctively, before I entered those ministries, I "covered" my family and loved ones with the blood of Jesus Christ. However, I failed to pray that my faithful secretary would also be covered. Soon after, she fell on the ice and required hospitalization for a month. My ministry (with all the people involved) had not been totally placed under the blood of Jesus Christ. It taught me a sober lesson. I trust I have learned it well.

The importance of Jesus' blood is very great. It

is so greatly important because it involves His person. (Genesis 9:4; Leviticus 17:14.) The present power of the blood of Jesus Christ is an extension of His own presence and power.

## Any Blood Will Not Do

It is not blood that makes the difference. Any blood will not do. It has to be the blood of Jesus. Jesus' blood is His life, His person, Himself. And He is God Almighty. There is power in the blood, power that is awesome indeed.

I have often seen the power of wind in uprooted, overthrown, destroyed trees. Those trees remind me of the power of Jesus' blood over the enemy. Satan's roots and life were destroyed by Christ's blood.

Jesus came to destroy the works of the devil (Acts 10:38). He did it with His blood. Note, for the first time in this study the blood is shown to have an offensive (as contrasted with defensive) power. It is a weapon of war.

Where Satan surreptitiously holds ground today, the present offensive, destructive powers of Jesus' blood need to be unleashed. Jesus is victor!

## Blumhardt's Battle

One of the longest known battles with demonic power took place in Germany when the godly Pastor Blumhardt waged lengthy and holy war against the demons which had invaded Gottleib Dittus, a young woman. The battle raged for two years. Thousands of demons were expelled. All kinds of unusual phenomena were observed.

Pastor Blumhardt was careful never to counsel the girl except in the presence of reliable witnesses. Finally, by persistent, prevailing prayer and by the destructive power of the blood of Jesus Christ, the strongholds of Satan were thrown down and the girl was liberated. Thereafter she became a teacher of children, and according to Blumhardt's testimony, was marked by "insight, love, patience, and kindness."[6]

## Win Power

As mentioned earlier, Jesus' blood has overcoming power. In Revelation 12:11 the saints are seen to overcome Satan "by the blood of the Lamb and the word of their testimony." There is "win power" in the blood of Jesus. The word from which "overcome" is derived is an old Greek battle term meaning "to conquer" or "to come off the field as victor." This truth is major!

And what is there to win? Or maybe we should ask, over whom do we have to win? There is a crown to win in the future and there is a battle to win over Satan—by the blood—now. Thank God the blood is incorruptible. Thank God it has present power.

Win power, now!

It is enough to make the believer recklessly jubilant. And perhaps that is why Jesus said "Rejoice not that the spirits are subject unto you, but rather rejoice because your names are written in heaven" (Luke 10:20).

# CHAPTER 6

### WEAPON #5:

# FASTING

*FASTING, THE DELIGHTFUL* discipline. Is this a contradiction in terms? Not so. Fasting can be truly rewarding in the life of a Christian. Fasting is geared for results. Far from somber truth dressed in drabness, fasting is a vibrant, radiant, yes, delightful Christian discipline.

But let's begin with an uncomfortable quotation from John Wesley, the founder of Methodism, in 1789.

> It would be easy to show in many respects the Methodists in general are deplorably wanting in the practice of Christian self-denial. While we were at Oxford, the rule of every Methodist was to fast every Wednesday and Friday in imitation of the primitive church.
>
> Now this practice of the primitive church

was universally allowed. "Who does not know," says Epiphanius, an ancient writer, "that the fast of the fourth and sixth days of the week are observed by the Christians throughout the world?" So they were by the Methodists for several years, by them all without exception. . . . The man who never fasts is no more on the way to heaven than the man who never prays.[7]

I must hasten to say that I do not wholly agree with Wesley's statement about a failure to fast keeping one out of heaven, because it cannot be backed up biblically. Nevertheless, it is fascinating that such a great man of God should make such an extreme statement about fasting. I take it that Wesley wanted no one to be in doubt about his opinion regarding this discipline. Possibly he used an extreme statement to make a needed emphasis and was not concerned that all he said about fasting be taken literally.

I have also heard fasting described as "the quickest way to get anything from God." I think that is absolutely true, though I would like to rephrase the statement to say, "Fasting is the quickest way to get yourself into the position where God can give you what He has wanted to give you all along!"

The late Dr. A.W. Tozer put it this way, "I fast just often enough to let my stomach know who's boss."

But what of the Scripture? The Bible has a

great deal to say about fasting. Some of it is exceedingly interesting—and some of it differs considerably from some popular ideas concerning this delightful but neglected discipline.

## Eighty Days for Moses

First, Moses practiced fasting (Exodus 24:18; 34:28; Deuteronomy 9:9, 18). On two occasions he fasted forty days without food or water, clearly supernatural fasts. The supernatural element is not the absence of food, but the absence of water. Ordinarily, a man without water will die in ten days. In addition, in Moses' case, the fasts were back to back, which means that if there was no break, Moses went 80 days without food and water. If this is the case, then Moses' 80 days without food was certainly supernatural. If Moses' fasting had been specified as the pattern for us, we could not hope to fast at all apart from God's supernatural intervention.

The human result from Moses' fasting was the reception of God's law among men, an event without parallel and nearly without equal in all of human history. The fasting played a significant part.

I cannot help further wondering what great events never happen because of our aversion to fasting.

## Variations

Elijah, too, was a man of the fast (1 Kings 19:8). Forty days and nights he went on the strength of his last meal. But the same statement, by its omission of any reference to drink, implies that Elijah did not abstain from liquids throughout the forty-day period.

And that in turn presents the possibility of variations in fasting: supernatural—like that of Moses—or natural—like that of Elijah (for it is well known that nearly everyone is able to abstain from food for forty days and live). Also, continuing to drink water while abstaining from food clearly demonstrates that fasts indeed are varied.

Elijah's ministry was dominated by the miraculous. There can be no substitute for the miraculous in the life of a Christian and fasting will unleash the supernatural.

Do you need a miracle? Fasting could be the door through which it will come.

## Daniel's Diet

Daniel's experience with fasting is fascinating (Daniel 9:3; 10:3). He fasted personally for twenty-one days. And apparently his fast was partial. He ate no pleasant bread nor flesh and drank no wine. But the Scripture stops short of saying he did not eat. From other references in the book of Daniel, it is possible to say that Daniel may have continued his simple diet. But he was fasting all the same, even if he was eating. Today, we would be inclined to call it dieting.

I do not know if you have noticed it or not, but as we have probed the Scripture, fasting has become more and more understandable and feasible. About this point some of you are asking, "Is it not a little much that this writer suggests that one can fast and eat at the same time?"

When I began to notice this possibility in Daniel, I went scurrying to a Bible dictionary. The definition was simple and clear. Fasting is a partial or total abstinence from food and/or water. Daniel and others in the Bible understood this.

Perhaps you cannot fast for many days. How about a few hours? Perhaps a partial fast will exactly meet your needs.

When you discover that it is possible to eat and fast at the same time, you are beginning to discover just how versatile fasting really is as a spiritual weapon. If fasting really is a spiritual weapon, anyone should be able to pick it up at any time and wield it in his own circumstances. And that is exactly the case.

## Grass-roots Fasting

The book of Jonah teaches about fasting as well. First, observe that the people proclaim a fast and the king supported it. Evidently the initiative for fasting can come from the grass roots as well as from those in authority. In the case of the Ninevites, the fast was total and even the animals were included. It lasted for three days and three nights and it was linked with repentance. Perhaps the greatest revival recorded in Scripture follows. The result was the salvation of a nation. And these Ninevites were not even acknowledged followers of Jehovah!

Can fasting be effective even when practiced by unbelievers? The Bible implies that it is possible. And if God answers the prayers of unconverted people (compare Acts 10 and 11 in the life of Cornelius), then why should God not honor the fasting of a repentant people?

## National Deliverance

The story of Esther demonstrates that a leader may also call a fast (Esther 4:16). Queen Esther called for a fast and all the people were obligated to cooperate. The fast was total for three days and three nights. But the Jews were delivered; the massacre of a nation was averted through the discipline of fasting.

Something similar to this may have happened in the 1973 overthrow of Salvador Allende, the Marxist president of Chile. One missionary was fasting daily during the breakfast hour for divine intervention in the affairs of the nation. On September 11, 1973, she felt the burden lift. (On September 11, 1973, the military coup took place.) And for the first time in many days the missionary began the day with breakfast. In my view, the events were related.

In the New Testament we read that Paul was in fastings (2 Corinthians 6:5). Note the plural. It is not surprising that our Christian experiences are not like those of Paul. Our fasting is not like his, either. Paul also says he was in fastings *often* (2 Corinthians 11:27). Frequent fasting has an obvious connection with spiritual power. But for most of us it is a connection that has been broken.

## Fasting without Hunger

In 2 Corinthians 11:27 (". . . in hunger and thirst, in fastings often") a fascinating truth about fasting comes to the fore. Paul distinguishes between hungerings and fastings. And if there truly is a difference between being hungry and fasting, then one of the most common objections to fasting is circumvented.

I recall looking forward with anticipation to a break in my evangelistic schedule. I wanted to fast for a few days. And can you imagine my delight when I discovered that from the very first there was no hunger?

Going hungry is one thing. Fasting is another. And once we learn that, fasting becomes an even more attractive and practical discipline. On the other hand, sometimes I find that I want to fast but cannot because I am too hungry, possibly because the Holy Spirit is not prompting the fast. But there are other times, when God wants me to fast, that it becomes to me the wholly delightful discipline that it is.

Our Lord and Savior, like Moses and Elijah, also fasted forty days. It is significant that He did this before His ministry began and before the miraculous began to occur. The absence of the miraculous among many of today's Christians could be traceable to the lack of this forgotten discipline.

I think it is also safe to assume that although Jesus did not eat for forty days, He did drink water. An indication of this is that Satan tempted Him on the point of eating, not drinking—on the point of hunger, not thirst.

## *Fasting Alone*

In Matthew 6, three fascinating promises are given (6:4, 6, 18). Christ says, "Pray, give, and fast in secret and God will reward you openly" (paraphrase). Fasting is here presented as a spiritual force in its own right. Praying brings results. Giving brings results. And fasting, by itself, brings results too.

Apart from prayer? Yes, apart from prayer. The promise which accompanies fasting is not hinged to prayer. It is hinged to fasting alone. Mind you, prayer and fasting are repeatedly linked in the Scripture. They are powerful twins in the spiritual warfare, but they are not Siamese twins. Together they multiply the release of spiritual power. But alone as well, fasting brings results.

Now any Christian would be foolish indeed to argue against praying. Far from it. But a word in favor of fasting needs to be spoken. A telephone operator, for example, who talks in her work, could be occupied completely with her job and could still apply tremendous spiritual force to a personal problem through fasting. And if she can maintain an attitude of prayer throughout, all the better.

## Missionary Fasting

Fasting in the book of Acts played a vital role in the commissioning of missionaries and in what we might now call church business meetings (Acts 13:1-4). Today we tend to schedule banquets when the church's business is to be done. Could that be why it is so poorly done sometimes? Could our lack of fasting have any relationship to the lack of missionary candidates?

Probably the greatest text on the subject of fasting is found in Isaiah 58:6. After a five-verse description of the type of fast God does not like, the prophet says, "Is not this the fast that I have chosen, to loose the bands of wickedness, to undo the heavy burdens and to let the oppressed go free, and that ye break every yoke?"

Fasting will loose the bands of wickedness. And there are plenty of those.

Fasting will undo the heavy burdens. And here is no shortage of burdened people.

Fasting will free the oppressed. And to me this is a clear reference to the liberation of those bound by Satan. Occult bondage is shattered by fasting. Sometimes nothing else will break through.

## Every Yoke

Fasting also will break every yoke. Thank God for that every. For example, an invisible yoke is often formed between a young couple, one a believer and the other not. Concerned parents talk and cajole. But arguments only push the young people together. Fasting is what is needed to break a yoke like that. And fasting can be applied to a problem without the participation or even the knowledge of the principals involved. Why, oh why, have we allowed the ruin of so many of our homes and families without ever once unsheathing the yoke-splintering fast which God has given us? The answer is not easy.

Christ made it clear that while He was present on earth His disciples would not fast, though the followers of John the Baptist, of course, did fast. But Jesus also made it clear that after He departed, His disciples would fast (Mark 2:19-20). I believe at Christ's return fasting by the church will be terminated. But now, in the meantime, fasting is God's order. A non-fasting church is out of order!

In any discussion of fasting some reference needs to be made to 1 Corinthians 7:5, "Defraud ye not one the other, except it be with consent for a time, that ye may give yourselves to fasting and prayer."

The context clearly indicates that a temporary abstinence from sexual relations within marriage is a fitting and proper self-discipline.

One of my friends in the ministry describes fasting this way: "Fasting is a disciplined abstinence from all that gratifies or satisfies the flesh in order to give one's self totally to seeking the Lord in the Spirit. This is the ultimate. Anything less is partial."

A fast may be undertaken in secret, as in Matthew 6, or it may be public, as in Acts 13. It may be initiated by a leader, as in Esther, or it may come from the grass roots, as in Nineveh. It may be done carnally, with wrong motives, and without effect. But if Christ truly lives in the church and in us, He is the same Savior who fasted forty days. And he wishes to express His fasting nature through us today so that He can hone the spirituality and discernment of His Church.

Some say, "I believe in fasting, but I don't feel led." It is true that we should be led as God's children. But why is it that so few Christians are led to fast when it is so obviously a vital part of Christianity? Usually, we fail to fast because the whole concept of fasting has remained uninviting and uninspiring. Fasting has not been presented as a wholly delightful discipline. But that is what it is!

## *Always Results*

At this point I would like to say I have never fasted without seeing some result. When I shared this fact with a friend who is a pastor, he countered with, "But when I fast, nothing ever happens."

However, we fasted together one day during a campaign and that evening the church was full. A film was shown which had a very ordinary impact. My message was ordinary enough, though evangelistic and clear. But God was there. There were many inquirers. Men, women, young people, and children. So many went to the inquiry room that we lost track of how many had responded.

The next day I asked my pastor friend, "Can you still say that God never does anything when we fast?"

With a smile, he answered, "No!"

## *A Last Word*

Enthusiasm for fasting is understandable. But the pitfall of regularly scheduled fasts should probably be avoided. All biblical fasts were issue-oriented. A determination to fast every Monday or the third Thursday, for example, may lead present-day believers into the kind of fasting the Bible consistently condemns. It is far better, I think, to apply the awesome power of fasting to specific issues at specific times. The results are certain to be gratifying indeed.

---

## CHAPTER 7

## Weapon #6:

# The Name of Jesus Christ

*Our world is* always impressed by big names. To be able to "drop" a big name is a status symbol among too many of us. Name-dropping may be nothing more than petty social maneuvering, but it demonstrates a basic human belief: names are important. And so there is the rush to "drop" the big names. This chapter zeros in on the biggest name of all, the Lord Jesus Christ.

If the prime minister or president of a country were to summon someone, it is most certain the citizen would respond and be present at the appointed time.

Even if the appointment should be at a very inopportune time, the average citizen would nevertheless rearrange his affairs so as to be present when the leader of his country wishes.

Yet these same citizens would be very un-cooperative indeed if an unknown Joe Blow should summon them for conversations in a far-off city.

The difference is a name. That is all. Names make the difference. Their importance cannot be overestimated especially in the kingdom of God.

In the Bible, names have tremendous significance. I would say that one who does not understand the significance of names cannot gain a basic understanding of the Scriptures.

In the spiritual warfare, in our struggles to win in the Christian life, "The name of the LORD is a strong tower, the righteous runneth into it, and is safe" (Proverbs 18:10). And not only is the name of our Lord a refuge and defense, it is also a weapon with devastating offensive power. The propitious use of the Lord's name makes things happen.

## Names Are Significant

In the Bible, other names also have significance. Adam and Eve are not just random phrases snatched out of the air to be used as labels on the first humans. Adam means "ruddy or red." And Eve means "life-giver." And so it goes, on through the pages of Holy Writ.

A good example of the significance of names is found in Judges 1:5-7. An obscure character named Adoni-bezek appears. His name means "lord of lightning." The Israelites caught him and cut off his thumbs and big toes.

Because his name suggests a relationship with Lucifer, who fell like "lightning" from heaven, I think it is a picture of the devil's defeat at the hands of Christians who take the offensive. Note that Adoni-bezek was defeated, not destroyed. The application is clear: Christians can wage a victorious warfare over Satan, the "lord of lightning"; they can get his thumbs and big toes, but God Almighty is the one who will finally send Satan to everlasting destruction.

Jacob's name, too, is especially significant. True to the meaning of his name, he was for years "the supplanter." Then after an all-night encounter with the Lord, Jacob's character was changed. (How many times have we excused ourselves by saying, "I can't help this; it is just the way I am"?) He became Israel, a prince with God.

To continue with references to names would fill this book and many others, but I believe you can see a principle established. Names are significant.

Our Lord, whose coming was prophesied in the Old Testament, was given a number of names before He was born, all of which describe in detail the character and ministry of the Savior. "And his name shall be called Wonderful, Counselor, The mighty God, The everlasting Father, The Prince of Peace" (Isaiah 9:6). In the New Testament our Savior is called a Lamb, the Lion of Judah, the Word, the Son of Man, the Son of God, and other names. Each one helps to describe the Lord Jesus Christ.

Another interesting and somewhat obscure sidelight in the Bible is that God's favor is attached to deeds done in the name of His followers. "He that receiveth a prophet in the name of a prophet shall receive a prophet's reward; and he that receiveth a righteous man in the name of a righteous man shall receive a righteous man's reward. And whosoever shall give to drink unto one of these little ones a cup of cold water only in the name of a disciple, verily I say unto you, he shall in no way lose his reward" (Matthew 10:41-42).

The name of a Christian disciple still has power. Since that is so, how much more power there is in the name of our Lord.

There are names, too, in the spirit world. The Holy Spirit has various names, none without significance. He is called the Comforter and the Spirit of Truth (John 14:16-17). Even the angels have names. Michael and Gabriel are two angels we know by name (Daniel 10:13, Luke 1:19). And Satan has other names, too. He is called the dragon, the serpent, and the devil (Revelation 20:2). The demons have names as well. Legion is the name of a demon referred to in the Bible (Luke 8:30) who apparently spoke for and represented several thousand associates. (A Roman legion was made up of three thousand to six thousand men.)

I do not think it appropriate to fill reams of paper with a discussion of demonic names, but sometimes a real key to deliverance of those subjected to the occult is to discover the names of intruding spirits. Evil spirits seem to be weaker when their names are known. The names can be discovered in three ways: direct revelation by the Spirit of God through the gift of discerning of spirits; a keen observation of the symptoms and bondage of the victim (for example, a person addicted to adultery may have a demon of adultery, though not always); and confrontation and probing. If there is spirit-speaking through the victim of demonic invasion, startling results can often be produced by demanding the name of the offending power "in the name of the Lord Jesus Christ."

## Unbelievers Use the Name

The name of Jesus Christ is very powerful. So powerful, in fact, that even unbelievers are able to use it effectively. Some will say, "Lord, Lord, have we not prophesied in thy name? And in thy name cast out devils? And in thy name done many wonderful works?" (Matthew 7:22). But Jesus will say to them, "I never knew you; depart from me, ye that work iniquity" (Matthew 7:23).

There are dangers when unbelievers try to harness the awesome power of Jesus' name. The sons of Sceva had a battle on their hands when they attempted exorcism without real faith in Jesus Christ. They escaped naked and wounded. Seven men were overcome by one demonized man (Acts 19:13-17).

In this section, however, I wish to focus on the name of our Lord Jesus Christ. (Our Savior deserves His full title. The more Christians learn about His name, the more inclined they are to use the full title.)

## Rescued Indians

"Jesus Christ's name saves from sin." These words are being written in the home of a missionary to the Cree Indians of Alberta. These people certainly need a Savior from sin. The night before last the missionary with whom I am staying had to take a wounded Indian to the hospital. Evidently his drunken brother had attacked him with an axe. At another of these same mission stations, drunken Indians once fired a rifle shot through a group of children coming home from a youth meeting. They had been shooting before they saw the children. Fourteen shots in all were fired. No one was hit, but one shot whistled right past the group of children and smacked into the side of a forty-five-gallon steel drum. Murder, adultery, drunkenness, and hate run riot in these parts.

But there is another side. Some of these Indians have been saved from sin. They are absolutely transformed, absolutely free. They used to do the same things their brothers do, but no more. Their bright eyes and radiant faces tell the story. Saved from sin by Jesus Christ! What a mighty name! "Neither is there salvation in any other; for there is none other name under heaven, given among men, whereby we must be saved" (Acts 4:12).

## *Explosive Results*

Jesus' name sets free from Satan, as we have already illustrated in this chapter. There is a reason why this is so. The name of Jesus Christ has lost none of its power. The authority and force of that name are undiminished. Centuries ago, Paul said, "I command thee, in the name of Jesus Christ, to come out of her" (Acts 16:18). The results were explosive then but are no less so today.

The name of Jesus also delivers from sickness. The man who was lame from birth was healed in the name of Jesus Christ (Acts 3:16). It certainly was not a healing effected by the intrinsic power of the disciples, though it did take place after Jesus Christ had ascended into heaven.

Peter and John were on the same footing as we are. Bereft of the physical presence of Jesus, by faith they dared to say, "In the name of Jesus Christ of Nazareth, rise up and walk" (Acts 3:6). I cannot help believe that if we dared to believe more, if we listened more carefully to the Spirit of God, if we were less afraid of hucksters and charlatans, we would certainly discover Jesus' name has lost none of its healing power.

## *Colombians Excel*

I enjoy Latin America and Colombia in particular. The Colombians are great believers. An evangelicalism without the preaching of divine healing is not likely to grow quickly there. The whole populace believes in the miraculous. And the faith of our brethren there has often shamed me.

I remember one time when a Colombian evangelist and I went to pray for a little grandmother who had been two years on her bed. I had no problem praying, but the Colombians excel in what comes next. They tell the sick to get up! And they do get up. Unfortunately, even after we had told the grandmother to rise and walk, she did not. And the next day, she did not want anyone to pray for her.

Later, after we had moved to the next campaign, a believer from the former town came to visit. I inquired about the *abuelita*. "Oh," he said, "she's walking all over." I was amazed but thrilled, too. I wish all our pastors in North America could take a course in divine healing in Latin America. These brethren have a lot to teach us, not the least of which is that Jesus' name delivers from sickness today!

## *Lay off the Name?*

A fascinating study of the name of Jesus Christ occurs in Acts 4. Such was the apostolic use of Jesus Christ's name that the authorities realized that the remarkable healing of the lame man had been effected by the use of the name of Jesus Christ. The authorities did not forbid preaching. All they wanted was for the disciples to lay off the name! Of course, the disciples would not. Peter and John knew where the source of their authority and power lay. They responded by asking for more healings, signs and wonders, all in the name of the holy child Jesus (Acts 4:30). Later, the apostles were beaten (Acts 5:40) because they would not stop using the name!

I further believe the biblical method for the preaching of the gospel is the use of the name. Philip preached the name and the kingdom (Acts 8:12). Paul also made it clear that to preach the gospel, so far as he was concerned, was to name Christ (Romans 15:20). Samaritan-style awakenings can still happen under the same style of preaching!

Jesus Himself hinges "the great commission " on His name. First, He told His disciples, "Go ye into all the world and preach the gospel . . ." (Mark 16:15). Then he told them what would happen—"And these signs shall follow them that believe; In my name they shall cast out devils; they shall speak with new tongues; they shall take up serpents; and they if they drink any deadly thing it shall not hurt them; they shall lay hands on the sick and they shall recover" (16:17-18).[8] All of this in His name.

Perhaps one of the reasons twentieth-century Christianity is so different from the first-century brand is our shrunken appreciation for the power and authority of Jesus' name.

Prayer, too, is linked to Christ's name. Jesus promised, "If ye shall ask anything in my name, I will do it" (John 14:14). He gave just one condition: His name.

## Lost Meaning

Many of us have a habit of ending every prayer in Jesus' name, whether we are saying grace at the table or "Now I lay me down to sleep. . . ."

Jesus' name has become so familiar that it has lost its meaning. But Jesus' name in the Scriptures is linked to God's glory (John 14:13). Ordination into the Lord's work and fruitfulness are intended to result in the effective use of Jesus' name. "Ye have not chosen me, but I have chosen you, and ordained you, that ye should go and bring forth fruit, and that your fruit should remain: that whatsoever ye shall ask of the Father in my name, he may give it to you" (John 15:16). I cannot help but feel there are some unplumbed spiritual secrets about the use of Jesus' name in prayer.

## Indiscriminate Praying

I must conclude that those Christians in church history and in the present time who have gained great effectiveness in prayer have at the same time discovered at least a tiny part of the full force of Jesus' name. When a prayer can genuinely be offered "in Jesus' name," that prayer is going to be answered. What may we conclude about all our unanswered prayers, except that we are making indiscriminate use of the mightiest name in heaven and on earth? May God forgive us—and teach us.

The name of Jesus meant that He was to save

His people from their sins (Matthew 1:21). The early disciples rejoiced that they were counted worthy to suffer shame for Jesus' name (Acts 5:41). Jesus made it clear, "And whoso shall receive one such little child in my name, receiveth me" (Matthew 18:5). The name of "Jesus" focuses on His person.

And that is where this whole study leads us. To the Lord Jesus Christ, the Person. His name is transcendent, "Wherefore God also hath highly exalted him, and given him a name which is above every name: That at the name of Jesus every knee should bow, of things in heaven, and things in earth, and things under the earth; And that every tongue should confess that Jesus Christ is Lord, to the glory of God the Father" (Philippians 2:9-11). Jesus' name implies the involvement of His person. That is why, when you properly use the name of the Lord Jesus Christ in spiritual warfare, the results are bound to be impressive.

Jesus Christ the Lord, the King of kings, intervenes personally on your behalf. He commits all that He is, all that He has promised, to your struggle, your difficulty. His name, properly applied, unleashes a whole series of events. His name makes things happen!

Christian soldier, put on your armor! Take up His almighty name! The transcendent name of the Lord Jesus Christ has power forever.

## CHAPTER 8

### WEAPON #7:

# TESTIMONY

"*AND THEY OVERCAME* him by the blood of the Lamb and by the word of their testimony . . ." (Revelation 12:11).

The Revelation saints of the last book of the Bible overcame Satan and the powers of darkness by the word of their testimony. And Christians today do the same. They overcome by their witness.

Why, we may properly ask, is testimony an overcoming weapon?

First, testimony is a spoken declaration to the world. "And with the mouth confession is made unto salvation" (Romans 10:10). What a man says is always significant. "By thy words thou shalt be justified and by thy words thou shalt be condemned" (Matthew 12:37). "For out of the abundance of the heart, the mouth speaketh" (Matthew 12:34). God often makes real to a man that which he dares to say with his mouth. "For verily I say unto you, That whosoever shall say unto this mountain, Be thou removed . . . those things which he saith shall come to pass; he shall have whatsoever he saith" (Mark 11:23).

So, I am saying, the very act of speaking our faith before Satan may be the whole difference between victory and defeat.

## A Powerful Factor

Second, experience is always a powerful factor in life. The man who was born blind had simply to say, "Once I was blind, but now I see." The proof was incontrovertible. The lame man who had lingered long years at the temple gates was up walking around. Even the apostles' enemies said, "We cannot deny it" (Acts 4:14, 16). Facts are stubborn, stubborn things—and devastating in their effect when God's power has been revealed.

Experience, nevertheless, is not a proper base upon which to build a theological structure. In Bible-believing circles these days there are two distinct types of literature. These two types are poles apart.

There are the experience books, the "this-happened-to-me-so-this-must-be-the-truth" type. The logic is faulty because the shifting sand of experience is converted into a launching pad for all kinds of theological missiles—many of them wildly off course.

Then there are the theologians who have every jot and tittle in place. They are saved, sanctified, justified—and all too often fossilized and maybe even petrified! The life and breath of the Holy Spirit of almighty God are nowhere to be found. The dispensations are all in place, but the men are not empowered. They are often devoid of the unction which ought to accompany the preaching of the Word of God.

Which extreme is worse I cannot say, though both are dangerous, and if I may say so, damning.

## *Screening out the Read-ins*

The safety of the middle ground is vital in our understanding of testimony. Testimony needs to be given in a context where a biblical basis for understanding exists, where theological and experimental "read-ins" are screened out. For example, if the lame man who was healed in Jesus' name had begun to teach others that because Peter said, "Silver and gold have I none," these same words must be uttered if anyone else expects to be healed, I would call that a read-in.

Each of the three times Paul gave testimony, he walked a careful line (Acts 22:1ff; 24:10-21; 26:1-27). Not once did he stray from a simple declaration of the acts of God in his own life.

Now I will admit experience sometimes leads men to truth. Nearly every servant of God has experienced events in his life which have led him to an understanding of Scripture. But it is better, I think, and the route is safer, to see the scriptural truth and then to have the experience.

And I repeat, testimony, when vibrant and

fresh, when based upon an act of God in one's life, is devastatingly powerful.

Some of the most memorable and most powerful gospel services I have ever been in have been services in which a testimony was given.

## Hammer Blows

Clarence Shrier, a Canadian friend of mine, was formerly a businessman and later a successful evangelist. He had a remarkable ministry of healing and prayer for the sick. The most powerful night in his crusades was almost always the last night, when he gave his testimony. He spent nine years upon a bed, was miraculously and divinely healed, and had a continuing ministry of healing for many years. He preached well and under great anointing, but the hammer blows of God's Spirit fell hardest when he gave his testimony.

Another friend of our family has a broken home. She reared her six children alone. In her lonely state she found Christ. But the abrasions and wounds of life have given her a powerful ministry in both music and spoken word. Her testimony, too, has tremendous power to convict and convert sinners.

Testimonies win victories over the enemy and minister to believers, too. I thank God for testimonies I have heard from the lips of true believers.

Nor should anyone be ashamed of the testimony God has given him. It may not be spectacular. It may, in part, be a story of failure and weakness. But people identify with weakness, with an individual and personal story, and they rejoice in the acts of God in the life of another.

There are times when silence is God's order. Often Jesus told those to whom He had ministered that they were to keep silent. Many times the people did not heed His word, but the Savior was nevertheless illustrating the principle of silence.

## Timing Must Be Right

Confessing Christ before men is certainly part of God's order. But the timing must be right. The rockets which tumble warplanes out of the sky have to be fired at precisely the right moment. So it is with testimony. Its premature delivery can make it a miss, when perhaps God intended a delay which would allow it to land right on target with tremendous, explosive power. (Taking time out now for a lengthy Bible study on God's timing would pay huge dividends!)

We need to know not only what the weapons are, but also how to become so sensitive to the Holy Spirit that our timing will be exactly right.

## Turning the Key

But there is side two to this record. There is a negative side to testimony—I call it confession. When a man tells the truth about his own sin to God or to offended brethren or to both, the results are also unusual.

I use the word "revival" carefully in my speech

and writing. I define a revival to be a mighty, renewing visitation of God Almighty which is so far beyond the usual, the ordinary, or even the greatly blessed events in the life of the Church that it must be called revival.

There have been few times in my ministry when I know I have seen revival—the Philippines and Africa come to mind. In every case the public confession of sin was the spark that kindled it. Prayer, preaching, and many other things play a part in revival. But the public confession of sin is the key. And so few care to turn it.

I have witnessed many confessions of sin, none of them without significance. However, one stands out in my mind. We were in Dedougou, Upper Volta, Africa. The atmosphere was one of brokenness and confession. The service could properly be called intense.

Then a missionary grandmother stood to her feet. She was petite and pretty. She had something very vital to say. "Please forgive me for not loving you as I should have," she asked the Africans. Her appeal was moving and sincere. She was touching and facing her basic offense.

Immediately, an elderly African named Levi stood up. Speaking for the group, he said something like this—"Yes, we forgive you. You are our mother. Our own mothers did not bring us the gospel. But you brought us the gospel. You are our mother."

The next thing we knew the missionary reached out and hugged that stately old man. Black and white together. Tears, oh so many tears.

Are you surprised that revival came? Revival always comes that way—through the confession of sins.

If we could fully know how much damage is done to the kingdom of darkness by confession, I am sure we would be more willing to confess our sins to one another.

## *Avoid Distortion*

Sometimes when Satan cannot stop the confession of sin he seeks to twist or distort it. In my judgment, the confession should be as large as the offense. If one person is involved, the whole church need not hear the confession. On the other hand, if someone has sinned against the whole congregation, then confession should be made to the whole congregation. In almost all cases of immorality and sexual deviation, confession should be private.

The teacher of an excellent seminar suggests that when pardon or forgiveness is asked, the one making the request should specifically ask to be forgiven. And then he should give opportunity to the offended person to do just that—to forgive.

Confession is biblical. "Confess your faults one to another. . . ." (James 5:16). Aaron confessed his criticism (Numbers 12:11). Saul made a false confession (1 Samuel 15:14, 25) and Saul still has his followers today. David confessed that he had "numbered" the people (2 Samuel 24:10). And Job, too, confessed his sin (Job 7:10; 42:6).

## Confessing the Sins of Others

Both Ezra (Ezra 9:6) and David (Psalm 9:20) confessed their personal sin and the sins of others. There is a sense, then, in which a leader, or a responsible person, can and may confess the sins of others.

One author, in his books dealing with occult bondage and deliverance, affirms that sometimes it is necessary for victims of demonic invasion to confess not only their own sins, but the "sins and subjections" of their forefathers. Frankly, I am inclined to agree with him. There are some cases when personal and corporate sins need to be confessed. Daniel confessed his own sins and the sins of his people (Daniel 9:5). We certainly know the iniquities of the fathers are visited upon the children to the third and fourth generations. Release from those sins and release from inherited or acquired demonic bondage can and does come through such confession and verbal, audible repudiation of the devil.

If our sins go unconfessed, our Lord will not hear us (Psalm 66:18; Isaiah 59:2). When we confess our sins it is Jesus Christ the Lord of glory who forgives them. "If we confess our sins he is faithful and just to forgive us our sins and to cleanse us from all unrighteousness" (1 John 1:9).

Inevitably these mighty weapons of the Christian warfare come finally to the person of Christ. A testimony? It is of what He has done. A confession? It is to Jesus Christ who alone can forgive.

And, my friend, if you are under pressure, pressed nearly beyond measure, almost without hope or strength in the battle, take courage. Positively affirm your faith. Audibly rehearse the acts of God in your life. Confess your sins. Confess them specifically and directly to God and to men when necessary.

And get ready. The results are likely to be explosive and obvious!

## CHAPTER 9

---

## WEAPON #8:

# FAITH

*MOST CHRISTIANS ARE* aware of the existence of the shield of faith mentioned in Ephesians 6:16. "Above all, taking the shield of faith wherewith ye shall be able to quench all the fiery darts of the wicked."

But not so many of our Lord's children remember that "by faith the walls of Jericho fell down" (Hebrews 11:30).

In fact, the whole "faith chapter" (Hebrews 11) is nothing less than a magnificent rehearsal of the offensive exploits of the faith heroes of the Bible.

It would be wrong to suggest that faith is not sometimes protective, even passive, within our hearts. But it will also take the offense. Faith will speak to the mountain and the mountain will move. Faith triggers events. The men and women of faith will often make things happen; in a positive sense, they can control events.

Regardless of what you face, Jesus says to you, "Be not faithless, but believing."

## *A Definition*

A passive definition of faith is this: to believe, to be persuaded of, to have confidence in, to trust in, to rely upon, to have entire dependence upon with assurance. To define faith is good, but not good enough. A full description and definition of faith can be gained only by a study of the Scriptures. And while this book cannot be exhaustive because of its nature and scope, we will focus on the Scriptures which reveal the "do-power" of faith.

The Christian life begins with an act of faith. "Believe on the Lord Jesus Christ and thou shalt be saved" (Acts 16:31). "For by grace are ye saved, through faith" (Ephesians 2:8).

To start to define it, we say that faith is the understanding of authority, accompanied by the willingness to act or rely upon it. The centurion who witnessed Jesus' healing ministry (Matthew 8:5-10) readily caught what many others had been oblivious to: Jesus healed through the function of authority. Being a military man himself, he was used to commands and instant obedience. Christ's ministry of healing and deliverance was not especially a prayer ministry. It was, instead, a ministry of authority, laced with commands.

Perhaps today, too, the ministry of healing (I speak only of that which is biblical and Christ-adorning) would be far different if authority and faith were properly linked.

## *Healing Evangelists*

The only people who come close to applying this practice are some of those who could be called the healing evangelists. They often simply pray and then command people to be healed. I am familiar with their work, especially in Latin America.

One of the most prominent of these healing evangelists visited Guatemala a number of years ago. A mission leader of fundamentalist persuasion, who was anything but pro-Pentecostal, nevertheless gave this account. When the evangelist preached, very large crowds gathered, and a large pile of crutches from those who were healed accumulated under the platform. From that campaign on, evangelical Christianity grew until it penetrated the whole country. Significantly, all types of evangelicalism benefitted.

I know all too well the abuses which have been associated with this kind of ministry. I know, too, that healing ability does not prove that a man is a man of God, or even that he is a true Christian. But still the principle used in many of the open-air healing crusades is a biblical one. Faith is understanding authority and acting upon it.

Faith also has some opposites: doubt, fear, unbelief. "Why are ye fearful, O ye of little faith?" (Matthew 8:26). That was the kind of question Jesus asked.

## *Measures of Faith*

The Bible also affirms that there are measures of faith. All men have faith—I speak of a basic human ability to believe. But such faith does not save anyone. Then there is saving faith. Some have great faith; some have little faith. Jesus suggested that faith no greater than a mustard seed could move mountains. Stephen was a man "full of faith." And Paul discussed the "proportion of faith."

The exciting thing, however, about all this is that faith can increase and does. Our faith can grow. "For therein is the righteousness of God revealed from faith to faith: as it is written, the just shall live by faith" (Romans 1:17). "Not boasting of things without our measure, that is, of other men's labours; but having hope, when your faith is increased, that we shall be enlarged by you according to our rule abundantly" (2 Corinthians 10:15). "We are bound to thank God always for you, brethren, as it is meet, because that your faith groweth exceedingly, and the charity of every one of you all toward each other aboundeth" (2 Thessalonians 1:3).

And the means of its growth is clear also. "So then faith cometh by hearing, and hearing by the word of God" (Romans 10:17).

Actually, the growth concept, relating to faith or any other principle, is one of the most exhilarating in the Word of God. No matter where we are in the Christian life, no matter what God has already done for us, there is more.

I recall hearing the late Dr. R.R. Brown of Omaha, Nebraska, speak at a convention in Winnipeg, Canada. What he said, I cannot recall. But for the first time in my Christian life, the growth concept fastened itself to my heart. I knew finally in my heart what I had known intellectually for a long time: There is always more with Jesus Christ. The jubilation in my heart was overwhelming.

## Y Hay Mas

In more recent years, I served as an interpreter for a Spanish Bible teacher from Argentina. His messages were profound and the blessing was great. But there was a recurring theme. Again and again he would say, *"Y hay mas!"* (And there's more!) Canadians were blessed by his ministry—and they even learned a little Spanish!

*Y hay mas!* And there's more! And there's more! So it is with faith. God's plan is that it should increase magnificently!

Faith also is affected by the adverse currents of unbelief. The disciples found themselves powerless to cast out a demon because of their unbelief (Matthew 17:19-20). When Jesus was about to heal a blind man (Mark 8:22-26), He took him outside the city. Some think it was to escape the unbelief in the city.

Jesus Christ, King of kings, Lord of lords, omnipotent God, the Author and Finisher of our faith, on one occasion could do no mighty miracles because of the unbelief of the people

Faith also has some vicarious characteristics. It can be exercised on behalf of others. When Jesus saw the faith of four men who had lowered their paralytic friend through the roof, He was moved to forgive and heal their comrade (Mark 2:5). The elders of the church, too, are able to offer prayers for the sick (James 5:15), and their faith results in healing.

I remember especially the first healing I was allowed to see in the ministry. And elderly shop keeper was deeply burdened for his wife who was sick in a city more than two hundred miles away. We slipped into a storage room and prayed together for his wife's deliverance. And she was healed! I was amazed. Sometimes I still am when God responds to faith.

## Faith You Can Catch

Another characteristic of faith is that it is communicable. It is contagious, if you will. Part of Paul's rejoicing over Philemon (Philemon 5-6) was that his faith was communicable.

One of the little understood factors about spiritual phenomena is that they are all contagious. The friendly assembly can easily turn into a frenzied mob when a spirit of riot invades the crowd.

Hate, fear, lust, alcoholism and homosexuality are not communicable diseases. But they are communicable spiritually. Occultism and spiritualism pass from generation to generation because they are spiritually transferrable.

Charismatic phenomena (a more pronounced presence in the church in recent years) are also communicable—both true and false.

In revivalistic and evangelistic movements there are rarely single conversions or renewals. More often in the kingdom of God there is a continuing chain of spiritual events. One thing always leads to another in the spiritual realm.

On the clearly positive side, faith is communicable. It is a spiritual intangible which can be both transferred and shared among people.

Frankly, most—if not all—of us must admit the faith in our hearts right now may well have come to us through spiritual contact with other followers of Christ.

Thank God for the household of faith! And away with unbelief!

## *Faith Can Deteriorate*

Faith can fail (Luke 22:23. Faith can be shipwrecked (1 Timothy 1:19). Faith must be built, maintained and strengthened continually.

Dr. Duane T. Gish, in debating for creation and against evolution, stresses the second law of thermodynamics (that all things are gradually running down or decaying) to test the evolutionary and creationist models. Man is very complex, says the professor, but when he dies he decays. To reverse this process, outside energy is needed. Plants grow by obtaining energy from the sun, but they require a complex energy conversion system. Dr. Gish also points out that the fossil records, instead of showing a gradual evolvement from the simple to the complex, show that "all systems change from the organized to the less organized."[9] If all things deteriorate, evolution cannot be right.

Faith, too, tends to deteriorate. And that gives reason enough for Christians to opt continually for the Word of God, which builds faith, and for Jesus Christ, who is the Source and Terminus of faith.

## Importunity—Sometimes

Another of the manifestations of faith is surely importunity. The Canaanite woman's daughter was healed because Jesus could not ignore her persistence and importunity (Matthew 15:21-28). And our Lord told her, "O woman, great is thy faith."

As is so often the case with scriptural truth, there are two sides to the coin. Sometimes one must simply ask God for what His Word promises and then believe. A layman in the Church of the Nazarene tells of receiving prayer for healing as a lad. Then he relates, "For several days I rolled on the floor with pain. I don't know what the pain was, but I knew God had healed my ulcers. When they had prayed for me, I was healed. Finally the pain stopped too." Nearly thirty years later he is well and vigorous, without ulcers. "What things soever ye desire, when ye pray, believe that ye receive them, and ye shall have them" (Mark 11:24). To believe is to receive. And for some, to pray a second time for something already requested is an act of unbelief.

At the same time, there are occasions when persistence and importunity will bring results which single prayers cannot. "So I tell you, keep on asking, and the gift will be given you; keep on seeking, and you will find; keep on knocking, and the door will open to you. For everyone who keeps on asking, receives; and the one who keeps on seeking, finds; and to the one who keeps on knocking, the door will open." (Luke 11:9-10, Williams Version) The context of this Scripture is importunity. And the Greek tenses of the text bear out the context—the key is keeping on.

In that notable and well documented case referred to earlier, Pastor Blumhardt warred against demons for two whole years before Gottleib Dittus was delivered.

George Mueller persisted in prayer for a whole lifetime, but it was not until after Mueller's death that some of his prayers were answered.

Faith, then, is sometimes evidenced in importunity. Great faith is never a stranger to importunity.

## Sometimes It Is Verbal

Faith must sometimes be verbal. Faith will speak before it sees. Testimony speaks afterward. Faith just speaks to the mountain. Jesus said, "If ye have faith as a grain of mustard seed, ye shall say unto this mountain, remove hence to yonder place; and it shall remove; and nothing shall be impossible unto you" (Matthew 17:20).

In a similar passage (Mark 11:23-24), saying is equated with believing. And Jesus clearly says, "he shall have whatsoever he saith."

When Dorcas died (Acts 9:40) Peter did not lay hands upon the body, nor did he anoint it with oil. Instead he "spoke to the mountain," and Dorcas was raised. Similarly, when Peter and John met the crippled man at the gate of the Temple, they neither prayed nor anointed. Instead, the spoken word was used—"In the name of Jesus of Nazareth rise up and walk" (Acts 3:6). The results were overwhelming. The mountain moved.

Sometimes the principles of verbalized faith can be applied to some very practical things. The ministry of our Christian newspaper was maintained very largely through the sale of books. During the writing of this volume we felt that one month we should ask for sales of $4,000. We talked about it publicly also. We verbalized our faith. By the end of the month the sales were $6,000.

The believer who knows he confronts a demon and dares to verbalize his faith will say, "You spirit, come out in the name of the Lord Jesus Christ!" He also will be much more successful than the believer who knows he confronts a demon but cannot bring himself to speak to it. All too often such a wavering believer asks the Lord in prayer to do something he himself has been commissioned to do (Mark 16:17).

Faith speaks. It speaks to the mountain. The principle is as old as creation. Elohim (the triune God) spoke and the worlds sprang into existence. Words spoken in perfect faith created the universe around us.

## *The Discipline of Silence*

But faith does not always speak. There are times when a man of God does not say all he knows. Instead, he maintains a discipline of silence. To betray that silence sometimes means that the faith is dissipated. It is as if God's confidence has been betrayed. Once you have seen that faith speaks, do not be so naive as to suppose that the Holy Spirit always works in the same way. "The secret of the LORD is with them that fear him" (Psalm 25:14).

Faith is action, too. When the ten lepers came to Jesus, He instructed them, "Go show yourselves unto the priests" (Luke 17:14). And as they went, they were cleansed. Faith, in their case, produced action, and in the process of the act of obedience, deliverance came. So faith sometimes is action.

The Syrophoenician woman said, "If I may touch but his clothes, I shall be whole" (Mark 5:28). She did it. She received healing, and she told others.

Of Goliath, David said, "I come to thee in the name of the LORD of hosts, the God of the armies of Israel, whom thou hast defied" (1 Samuel 17:45). David did it too. He ran to meet Goliath.

He hurled the stones. He cut off the giant's head. He received. And others told it. "Saul has slain his thousands, but David has slain his ten thousands."

The prodigal son said, "I will arise and go to my father" (Luke 15:18). He did it too. He received forgiveness. And the onlookers told it. So well did they tell it, that the elder brother got angry and upset.

## Ultimately It Is Jesus

Any discussion of faith must ultimately focus on Jesus Christ. He is the author of it and the finisher of it (Hebrews 12:2). Whatever your needs are, they are met in Jesus Christ. Whatever the impossibility you face, our Savior is the full and adequate answer. His promises are enough. "For all the promises of God in him are yea, and in him Amen" (2 Corinthians 1:20). "But my God shall supply all your need according to his riches in glory by Christ Jesus" (Philippians 4:19).

Faith could be described almost indefinitely, but this is not a book about faith. It is enough to remember that Jesus said, "all things are possible to him that believeth?" (Mark 9:23).

Someday, somebody, somewhere is going to really believe that Scripture. That man or woman will change the world.

# CHAPTER 10

---

## Weapon #9:

# *Unity*

*"I NOW PRONOUNCE* you husband and wife." These are momentous words, romantic words, dramatic words, beautiful words. And those of us who have stood before a minister in the marriage ceremony will never forget them.

They are powerful words, too!

If the Bible is to be taken seriously (and I do take it that way), then one shall chase a thousand but two who have become one will put ten thousand to flight. Marriage is divinely instituted, corporate power.

Such unity power is never far removed from the pages of Holy Scripture. We find a corporate ministry in creation in the very first verse of the Bible. "In the beginning, God created. . . ." The word used for God is Elohim, a plural noun. And since Hebrew nouns can be singular, dual or plural, the very first verse of the Bible teaches that creation was accomplished by the Trinity, working together in unity.

When man was created. God said, "Let *us* make man in *our* image" (Genesis 1:26, italics mine). Creation itself was an act of unity. The creation of man, the highest act of God's creation was also an act of unity, an act of the Trinity.

When a stop had to be put to the tower-building at Babel, God said, "Let *us* go down and there confound their language" (Genesis 11:7, italics mine).

Creation and judgment, both mighty manifestations of God's power, were acts of unity—demonstrations of divinely instituted corporate power.

## Spiritual Power Structure

Human marriage, to which we have already referred, is a physical union, but it is more—it is a spiritual power structure. For example, when continence within marriage is agreed upon, it defeats Satan (1 Corinthians 7:5). Husband and wife are heirs together of the grace of life (1 Peter 3:7).

These facts being so, Satan wars against marriage. Divorce is his victory. Not surprisingly, he also campaigns to keep the unmarried single if he realizes that God's plan for that person includes marriage. (Marriage, of course, is not always God's plan.) The enemy campaigns vigorously and continuously against marriage, either to block it from happening or to ruin it after it has taken place, because he sees it as it is: a spiritual power structure that blocks his path to ruining mankind.

We should be thankful for the spiritual power that is locked into this most basic human experience of oneness, marriage.

Unity is especially important in warfare and this is made exceptionally clear in the Bible. Moses wrote, "And five of you shall chase an hundred and an hundred of you shall put ten thousand to flight" (Leviticus 26:8). Saul's great warriors were of one heart (1 Samuel 10:26). Jonathan and his armor-bearer, both valorous men, were as one (1 Samuel 14:1-17). The great soldiers of the Old Testament were successful because they understood the necessity of unity.

## Divided We Shall Fall

These lines are written in an era when the western democracies had allied themselves against communist armies and ideologies. Unity before a common enemy has vanquished that enemy and preserved freedom until this day,

What was true on the battlefields in Joshua's day is true in the nuclear age. And the generals of the twentieth century know it.

What is less generally known is that the principles of unity especially apply to spiritual warfare. Striving together in prayer brings deliverance (Romans 15:30). "If two of you shall agree on earth as touching any thing that they shall ask, it shall be done for them" (Matthew 18:19).

If two men cannot even walk together except they be agreed (Amos 3:3) the absolute importance of unity surely must be understood. It is good for brethren to dwell together in unity (Psalm 133:1). One of the dominant themes of Paul's writings in the New Testament is togetherness (Ephesians 1:10; 2:5-6; 2:21-22; 4:16).

The principles of unity also apply to Christian experience. Before the early believers were filled with the Holy Spirit, they continued with one accord (Acts 1:14). When they were later filled with the Holy Spirit they were again, or perhaps still, of one accord (Acts 2:1). Later, being together, having all things in common, they continued daily in corporate worship, and God was pleased to give them evangelistic effectiveness (Acts 2:45-47).

## A Corporate Cry

In the fourth chapter of Acts, the setting was similar. First there was unity and a corporate cry toward God (4:24). Then they were filled anew with the Holy Spirit (4:31). When they were all of one accord in Solomon's porch, signs and wonders were done in Christ's name (Acts 5:12). When Philip the evangelist preached Christ in the power of the Holy Spirit, there was a positive, united response (Acts 8:6). Later the first missionaries were sent out by men in agreement.

The conclusion is inescapable. Operations of the Holy Spirit which involve a community of persons require an atmosphere of unity. And that unity coordinates the unleashing of God's power. And when unity power is demonstrated, the results are likely to be obvious.

Therefore, a small group of Christian believers which is marked by complete unity will certainly have more spiritual power than will a badly divided congregation of eight hundred.

## Group Experiences

Another basic observation needs to be made. If unity unleashes spiritual power, then unusual spiritual experiences are not reserved for individuals. Nor are all the mighty acts of God for the closet. There is such a thing as a corporate spiritual experience. A whole group may experience together a work of the Holy Spirit which God Almighty has planned for it.

The arrival of this truth to my heart was timed perfectly—before an overseas trip to Mali, Upper Volta, and the Ivory Coast.

At a place called Bono in Mali, sixty-three African preachers plus several missionaries, all of the Christian and Missionary Alliance mission, gathered together. From the very first the meetings were marked with brokenness and confessions. For several days we met, and one by one the Christian workers made peace with one another and with the Lord.

The symbol of forgiveness in that tribe is the stretching forth of both hands. On the last day of the conference at about four in the afternoon, we finally arrived at the place where all of us—more than sixty men (and one woman!)—could all extend our hands to each other. We were of one accord.

I know I had never before preached to a congregation so thoroughly right with one another. My text was the proper one—Acts 2. And the message was one of the briefest I have ever delivered. Essentially it was this: The Holy Spirit wants to fill us. We need to be filled. The phenomena vary. The tongues of flame, the wind, the speaking in other languages was God's way in that day. Today God can repeat any, all, or none of those signs. But he does want to fill us. We will know, feel and hear.

## Marked Forever

Then we had simple, corporate prayer which included the words, "Fill us with the Holy Spirit." That was all. Then the Holy Spirit came upon us. Audibly. And when He began to manifest Himself, He immersed us in a veritable ocean of love. He washed our eyes with tears. He poured joy into us! I believe most of us were marked forever that day. I was. The Holy Spirit had given us our own Pentecost. Unity was the key. And if the details of that mighty day all fade from my mind, I will still remember one thing: I saw the power of unity. The power of unity is well known to Satan. He fears Christian unity and labors mightily and tirelessly to short circuit or destroy it by uniting his own workers against it.

The unity of evil at the tower of Babel triggered God's judgment (Genesis 11:5-8). When the evil and the righteous are joined in marriage, the tendency is toward evil (Genesis 34:16-22). Ananias and Sapphira agreed together to tempt the Lord (Acts 5:9) and Peter made it clear that Satan had filled their hearts. When Stephen was murdered (Acts 7:57), he was martyred by evil men in one accord. In the book of Revelation the strategy of evil is the same: the ten kings have one mind to give their power and strength to the beast (17:13).

## Pay Attention!

We had better pay attention and we had better believe the devil knows the power of unity. He seeks to destroy it in the kingdom of God and he seeks to harness it in the kingdom of darkness. It is time we realized our agreeing power is devastating on the offense. "If two of you shall agree on earth as touching any thing that they shall ask, it shall be done for them of my Father, which is in heaven" (Matthew 18:19).

Believers are united with Christ. We are one with Him in death and resurrection (Romans 6:5). We are part of His body (Romans 12:4-5).

The human spirit becomes one with the Holy Spirit when we are joined to the Lord (1 Corinthians 6:17).

Christ himself was and is and always shall be one with the Father (John 10:30; 17:21).

But if we are believers, if we are one with

Christ, then surely our Savior is trying to teach us that the "throttle of omnipotence" is in our hands.

Stagger if you will at such a thought. As for me, with God's help I do not want to be among those who stagger—I want to dare to think God's thoughts God's way. United with Him, we will partake of His life. He is the Vine. We are the branches.

Oh, to believe it, to discover the power of unity, and to use it for His purposes!

---

## CHAPTER 11

**WEAPON #10:**

# *BELIEVER'S AUTHORITY*

*AUTHORITY MIGHT BE* called the powerless power because the one exercising it has no power in himself. The power of authority also varies. The local policeman has authority, as does the prime minister or president. Their powers, though, are not equal, nor necessarily of the same quality.

Now when we talk about the authority of the Christian believer it must be said that he himself has no power. But the authority vested in him—and which is intended to flow through him—is omnipotence itself.

And if that doesn't keep you reading, nothing will!

### *Authority Levels*

In the Scripture's view of the world, authority levels are always evident. Creation itself demonstrates authority. The lion is the king of the beasts and everything else turns aside for him (Proverbs 30:30). That means that if a lion meets a dog on a path, the dog will turn aside. As would a cow, an elephant or an ostrich. Authority (and perhaps survival) makes it so.

Now if a cow meets a horse on the path, again one must turn aside. It will be the cow (unless she is angry!) and the authority structure in the animal world is the reason. If perchance a cat meets a dog on the trail, the cat will always turn aside, unless the dog is too tiny or the cat is angry! I do not think there would ever be a question about what would happen if a cat should meet a mouse on the trail. Either self-preservation or hunger would surely prevail!

Even among animals of the same kind there are levels of authority. When I was a boy we had a cow named Nancy. She was sloe-eyed, deceptively low slung, and indisputably the boss (or should I say belle?) of the barnyard. When new cows joined the herd, she battled them into submission. When the dogs threatened her calf (or any other cow's calf) she charged off to do the battle. She was the only cow I ever saw who had a personality and a conscience. And it was a sad, sad day when Nancy went to market.

But I learned some memorable lessons about authority from Nancy, and perhaps you will, too. I am persuaded that if we can see God's authority structure function in nature, we will find ourselves apt and ready to understand and experience the authority of the Christian believer.

## Authority over Animals

Man has been given "dominion" or authority over the animal world (Genesis 1:26; Psalm 8:5-8). Again, because this world is sin-contaminated, there are exceptions, but man does have authority over the hungry lion if he cares to extend it.

A child may walk into a herd of cattle and though the child weighs no more than forty pounds and the animals an average of six hundred pounds each, the herd will divide to give way before that tiny human being. The reason is man has authority over animals.

The farmer in the middle of a field has authority over the angry bull charging him. But if he is not prepared to exert that authority, he had better climb the nearest tree!

The woman who is confronted with a tiny mouse in her living room has authority over the wee thing. But I am not sure she always is willing to get down off the furniture to exert it.

Still, God has given man authority over animals—the exceptions only prove the rule.

## And One Another

Men also exert authority over one another (Matthew 8:9-13). The centurion who talked with Jesus understood this. The mayor of the city, the chairman of the board, the president of the company, the husband of the home, all have positions of authority, and we understand that well.

Without these basic authority structures there would be anarchy and chaos. We cannot even imagine an army without a structure of command.

And I hasten to add, if we can understand the function of human authority we will easily grasp the principles of the believer's authority.

## *Spiritual Forces*

Above the levels where human authority exists, there is a spiritual realm occupied by spiritual forces. There are spirit beings who, through the fall of man in Eden, have gained a place where they are able to dominate man. I doubt that an evil spirit could ever gain dominance over a man who had never sinned. Unfortunately, every man is a sinner and thus vulnerable.

Jesus (in Luke 13:11) confronted a spirit which had bound a woman for eighteen years. The satanic power had somehow gained control over her and had held it for all those years. I am not suggesting she was necessarily victimized because of her own sin. But Adam's sin certainly was an antecedent to her bondage.

Paul confronted a spirit of divination which had gained control over a young girl. That spirit was dislodged in Jesus' name (Acts 16:16).

But those demonic spirits are themselves under authority. Satan is the head of a vast hierarchy of principalities, powers, rulers, and forces of spiritual wickedness in high places (Ephesians 6:12). How many levels there are in this system we do not know. But the Bible does speak of the

Prince of Persia (Daniel 6); hence there may be satanic underlings who have specific authority over geographical areas of the world. We do know that Satan is neither omnipotent, omnipresent, nor omniscient. And because Satan has to "go about" his worldwide kingdom of darkness, his projects and activities must necessarily be carried out by subordinates or underlings.

In the last paragraph I introduced two additional authority levels which upon the testimony of Scripture do exist. Those who have with any frequency been involved in a ministry of deliverance and exorcism will verify what has been stated here. The names and ranks of demons is an investigation which, though enlightening and real enough, tends to bring an unhealthy focus on Satan who is properly and significantly called the prince of this world. For that reason, we will not pause here.

### The Believer's Authority

The next level of authority may surprise you—it is that of the believer. If we diagram what we have been saying so far, it will appear something like this:

The moment a man believes in Jesus Christ he changes position in the diagram. Whether he feels it or not, he is above the enemy. This is represented by the arrow.

If there is one page Satan would like to tear out of the Bible, it is the one on which these words were written to early Christian believers: "And [God] hath raised us up together, and made us sit together in heavenly places in Christ Jesus" (Ephesians 2:6). Colossians 2:10 further describes the believer's position: "And ye are complete in him which is the head of all principality and power." And we must not forget the tremendous revelation of Colossians 2:15: "And having spoiled principalities and powers, he made a shew of them openly, triumphing over them in it."

## Game Over

Jesus Christ, through the power of his death and resurrection, asserted and now maintains this position of authority. For Satan, it is already "game over."

Now the delightful, awesome, even staggering truth is that the Christian believer, by virtue of his position in Jesus Christ, shares the Savior's total dominance and mastery over Satan. That is the reason why believers are the only ones who can confront the demonized and deliver them. "These signs shall follow them that believe; In my name they shall cast out devils" (Mark 16:17). And may I repeat, the believers are successful by virtue of their position in Jesus Christ and His authority which flows through them.

The tendency upon discovering the immense power in the believer's authority is often to be unduly fascinated by it. Certainly it is an awesome thing, and for that reason, I am sure, Jesus said, "Rejoice not, that the spirits are subject unto you; but rather rejoice, because your names are written in heaven" (Luke 10:20).

## Witch Hunting

It needs also be said that a deliverance ministry should never, never become an end in itself. Contemporary church history is strewn with the wreckage of good ministries which have been deflected into witch hunting and other hurtful emphases. The man who sets up a deliverance center and invites everyone to come to him with their demon problems will get far more than he bargains for. Deliverance is intended to follow, not lead, the preaching of the Word of God (Mark 16:20). A ministry which attaches any more than a peripheral interest to deliverance is a ministry which is threatened.

## Other Avenues

There are other avenues of Christian authority. I have met Christian brothers who are greatly blessed in praying for the sick. Invariably they understand that Christ's authority over disease has been extended to them (Matthew 10:1).

In addition, it is clear from Scripture that the ministry of leading new believers into the fullness of the Holy Spirit is one of authority. Simon the sorcerer may have had bad motives, but he did recognize that Peter and John had a ministry of authority (Acts 8:19, 9:17). Through the apostolic ministry of authority, the Samaritan believers were filled with the Holy Spirit.

## Binding and Loosing

However, the area upon which I would like to focus so far as the believer's authority is concerned is that of binding and loosing.

In Matthew 12:29 Jesus says, "How can one enter into a strong man's house, and spoil his goods, except he first bind the strong man? And then he will spoil his house." From the context it is clear that Satan is the strong man. Thus the lines are drawn. For effective spiritual warfare, for victory over the enemy, we must first bind the strong man. Then we can spoil his house. All too often, attempts are made to brush by the strong man to get at the work of the Lord. And just about as often, we are frustrated.

Peter was one of the first who was given this authority, "And I say also unto thee, That thou art Peter, and upon this rock I will build my church; and the gates of hell shall not prevail against it. And I will give unto thee the keys of the kingdom of heaven: and whatsoever thou shalt bind on earth shall be bound in heaven: and whatsoever thou shalt loose on earth shall be loosed in heaven" (Matthew 16:18-19).

For too long we have busied ourselves explaining why Peter did not have special authority. I think all this has been in reaction to the interpretation the Roman Catholics have given to this passage, making Peter the first pope and leader of the Church. Even before I understood what I do now, I was never satisfied with the traditional Protestant interpretations of this passage. My rule of interpretation for the Scriptures is this: If the literal sense makes common sense, seek no other sense. And, for the life of me, I cannot see why we should feel theologically threatened if we admit that Peter actually was given authority to bind and loose, to forbid and allow. That in no way is a declaration that Peter was a pope, nor that he was infallible.

## Not Only Peter

Our fears and reactions are especially unnecessary because Jesus extended his authority of binding and loosing to all of his disciples. He said, "Verily I say unto you, Whatsoever ye shall bind on earth shall be bound in heaven: and whatsoever ye shall loose on earth shall be loosed in heaven. Again I say unto you, That if two of you shall agree on earth as touching any thing that they shall ask, it shall be done for them of my Father which is in heaven. For where two or three are gathered together in my name, there am I in the midst of them" (Matthew 18:18-20).

A careful reading of the Greek tense requires that verse 18 be understood this way: "Whatsoever you bind on earth is that which is already bound in heaven, and whatsoever you lose on earth is that which is already loosed in heaven." A friend puts it this way, "The believer does not exercise this authority according to his own reasons or whims; rather, by the Holy Spirit's leading, he is simply cooperating with the divine will in any matter."

## We Fail to Believe

We evangelicals vigorously claim the promises of verses 19 and 20. We believe that if two agree, it shall be done! We believe where two or three people are gathered together in Christ's name, He is there too.

By what logic, then, do we fail to believe that whatever we bind will be bound and whatever we loose will be loosed? Part of the reason for our failure is that we stagger at the thought. Is God really putting the throttle of omnipotence into our hands? In one sense, He is!

Binding and loosing are not indiscriminate any more than prayer is indiscriminate. They are aligned with heaven. Binding and loosing need to be controlled by the Holy Spirit as much as prayer.

## You Do It

Jesus said, "Whatsoever *ye* shall bind" (italics mine). You do it. Binding and loosing are not prayer. If you read this section and commence to pray, "O Lord, bind Satan," you have missed the whole lesson! The day is coming when the Lord will bind Satan and he will be cast into the abyss. But in the meantime believers must do the binding. If you believe, you do it! "I bind. I loose." These are the words of authority.

Binding and loosing need to be verbal, preferably out loud. And they need to be specific. Say exactly what you mean and mean what you say. I once was involved with a group of Christian workers in a case where no solution seemed possible until we were willing to loose what had been inadvertently bound and then re-bind it. It was a lesson, believe me, in the necessity of speaking specifically and exactly in binding and loosing.

## A Prayer Rut

I recall a dear Christian brother who heard me share this material. He had developed a prayer rut in which he regularly asked the Lord to bind Satan. I carefully and deliberately told the study group that binding and loosing were believers' prerogatives and responsibilities. I also said that if people continued to say, "O Lord, bind Satan," they would have missed the whole point of my teaching.

My brother listened carefully enough. So I wondered what his prayer would be like. If a prayer can be funny, his was, because he slipped in and out of his favorite prayer rut, he garbled his words, but he could not bring himself to seize the throttle that was available to him.

He had missed the whole lesson.

The policeman on a traffic stand does not pray,

"O Lord, in the name of the city fathers, please stop this traffic." That is so absurd as to be ridiculous. But many Christians today are very much like such a policeman. They cannot bring themselves to just stop the traffic. They cannot bring themselves to believe that the throttle of authority is really in their own hands.

## Other Examples

There are some biblical illustrations which lend additional insight here. In Mark 11:1-16 the colt had to be loosed for Jesus' use. Now Christ's supernatural power certainly was sufficient to bring that colt spontaneously to His side or even to create a colt for the job. Instead, He sent His disciples to do the loosing. There was the economy of the miraculous. The Savior did only what was necessary! He described the colt and its location. But He left something for the disciples to do. Loose the colt. And they did it.

Jesus also raised Lazarus from the dead, even after the process of decay had set in. But though he unleashed His resurrection power into Lazarus' corpse (John 11:39-48), there also was the economy of the miraculous. If Christ could raise the dead, He certainly could have snipped the grave clothes into a thousand pieces. But He chose not to do it. Lazarus had to shuffle forth and then the disciples had to loose him.

Spurgeon believed, and I heartily concur, that there are many like Lazarus in the church today. They are alive, but still hampered by grave clothes. They need to be loosed! Loosing them is a disciple's ministry.

In Luke 13:10-16, Jesus loosed a woman from a spirit of infirmity which had gripped her for eighteen years. Paul and Silas were in prison, but through praise their bonds were loosed (Acts 16:26). Isaiah, too, apparently sensed the necessity of loosing. He declared the loosing power of fasting. (Isaiah 58:6).

## A Warning

I wish to conclude this chapter with some helpful illustrations, but I must first give a warning. If binding and loosing is a ministry directed against Satan, and I think it is, then extreme caution needs to be exercised. As Dr. Tozer once observed, "The devil knows more judo than you've ever heard of." We must remember that in disputing about Moses' body, even Michael, the archangel, did not dare bring a railing accusation against Satan (Jude 9). Any believer who is so foolish as to think he can taunt Satan will certainly get trouble, and lots of it. On the other hand, no believer sensing his absolute authority in Jesus Christ should ever fear the enemy.

## Binding a Bar

On one occasion a friend of mine was ministering near the border of one of the southern states. A new bar was about to open across the state line. It was erected, finished and furnished—but not yet in use.

When my pastor friend learned of the situation, he sensed the bar was a threat to the work of the Holy Spirit in his area. So he and his wife, along with a young man, drove into the yard where the building was located. Sitting in their pick-up truck, they joined hands and audibly in the name of Christ forbade the bar ever to open. And it didn't!

Whatever you bind, or forbid, including bars, will be bound. The key, of course, is to keep earth and heaven in tune, to be controlled by the Holy Spirit. Then what you "say," you will have. "Bind" and "loose" have the meanings of "forbid" and "allow."

## Breaking Blockades

A few years ago in the small town where we lived there was a farmers' strike or, more properly, a blockade, in which pickets took up positions to stop delivery of farm produce to the processing plants. Because our family owns a seed-processing plant we were involved. Some of the agitators were quite revolutionary and tempers flared. Violence threatened. The air in that small town seemed charged with hate and fear.

Finally, late one night, I came to a spiritual realization. The forces abroad in our town were evil. I lifted my hands toward the starry sky in my backyard and said something like this: "Lord, in the name of Jesus Christ I come against these forces and I break their power and bind them completely. And I loose the flow of seed into the plant."

The very next day a judge in Calgary, Alberta, told the agitators their strike was illegal and their goals ridiculous. That very day seed began to flow into the plants.

A few days passed and we noticed that no seed was flowing into a plant our family owns in a nearby city. I had forgotten to include that plant in the loosing. There was another prayer-and-loosing session and the seed began to flow there too. If you believe, as I do, that the invisible is more real than the visible, you will be inclined to agree that binding and loosing can be very practical indeed.

I limit my illustrations to three, but if you are spiritually perceptive you will see that binding and loosing can indeed apply to any—literally any—situation. Like the "whatsoever" Jesus used to teach about prayer, He used a "whatsoever" to teach about binding and loosing.

## An Adamant Man

A few years ago, I was invited to a town in Montana. There the young pastor had been laboring faithfully. But one man, a backslider, had rejected the pastor's efforts. He was adamant. "I'll never go back into that church again," he vowed. The pastor understood binding and loosing because he had so persistently loosed the man from his backsliding. (There's a teaching tidbit right here—binding and loosing can be continual and repetitious.) He was so sure the man was going to return to his spiritual moorings that he had taken a 3x5 card and written a date plus words to the effect that the man in question was "loosed today."

All through the special meetings we prayed and loosed. We went to visit the backslider several times. But it seemed that each time we went he was watching a football game on his television set. We were after the man's soul, but we couldn't get the TV off! Finally we came to the last day, a Sunday. The man was not there in the morning service and so after lunch I phoned him.

"Will you come to the service tonight?"

"I will."

Later, as he milked cows he told his wife he was going to church. "But if those two preachers get on my back," he added, "I'll just bolt out of there."

The evening service came and the man strode into church. He listened to the gospel as if he had never heard it before. When the invitation was given he was the first to respond. Others followed him until the front pew of the church was filled with inquirers. We prayed with each one.

But when I came to speak to that backslidden brother, all I felt in my heart to say was simply, "Brother, in Jesus' name, I loose you. I loose you."

Immediately he said, "I take it. I take it."

When I looked into his eyes there seemed to be a lack of assurance, but his words were positive.

I let him return home without ministering to him further. But I was uneasy. "He wasn't really clear in his eyes; he needs more help."

In prayer, the pastor and I kept on loosing our brother. I cannot recall if both of us went to his home once more or not, but at least one of us did.

The news was fabulous. "When I got home," he said, "I put on my pajamas and went into the living room to kneel down and pray. When I knelt down, all of a sudden, the Lord set me free. If God fills me any fuller it will blow a hole in my chest!"

He was a man who had been loosed. It seemed, indeed, that no other ministry had been effective. God help us not to stagger at any of His promises.

## Based on Fact

Now all this teaching, this whole section, is based on a basic theological fact: Jesus Christ is far above all principalities and powers. We are in Jesus Christ and seated with Him in heavenly places (Ephesians 1:20-22; 2:6). Each and every one of these tremendous spiritual weapons begins and ends in Jesus Christ.

To live and experience Jesus Christ is, among many other things to exercise His power—to let it flow through us.

Some will be afraid. They do not believe it can really be true that such authority is committed to the believer in the Lord Jesus Christ.

Like rookie policemen with uniforms, badges, and training, they stand quaking at the curb. They are sure if they have to stride out into the traffic and hold up their hands, nothing will happen.

But because of Jesus Christ the traffic will halt. If you call a halt to the forces of darkness they will—they must—obey.

Isn't it time we stepped off the curb and into the flow of life's traffic—out where the needs are? I think so.

Yield yourself completely to the Holy Spirit's control. Believe. Act. What happens will be awesome indeed!

## CHAPTER 12

## WEAPON #11:

# THE GIFTS

*THERE ARE SOME* things, I believe, which God intends to do for you in your Christian life, but which He will not be able to do except through a charismatic channel.

If you are like I am, you are caught in a worldwide charismatic controversy. The gifts are assiduously promoted as a cure for all that ails the church. Or they are vigorously denounced as the source of all kinds of evil.

As I have written in *The Third View of Tongues*, "there has to be a middle ground."[10] There needs to be a third view of the charismata. And though in the scope of this one brief chapter no exhaustive statements can be made, I am persuaded, nevertheless, that an emphasis on the charisma belongs here. Many mighty events wait to happen in our day. The charismatic abilities of the Christian church will unleash them.

There are great lessons which are untaught because good and godly men have not possessed God's gifts of teaching.

There are miracles which are waiting to happen because God's children are not sensitive to the Holy Spirit's plan to work miracles today.

There are those who are bound by Satan who are not likely to gain their freedom apart from the function of the gift of discerning of spirits.

There are great churches waiting to be founded and led by men with the gift of pastor-teacher.

And we could go on.

By the word "charisma" I mean particularly the position gifts and power gifts that the Holy Spirit has given to the church.

These lists are found mainly in three Scripture passages: Romans 12:6-8; 1 Corinthians 12:7-11, 28; and Ephesians 4:11-12.

"Having then gifts differing according to the grace that is given to us, whether prophecy, let us prophesy according to the proportion of faith; or ministry, let us wait on our ministering; or he that teacheth, on teaching; or he that exhorteth, on exhortation: he that giveth, let him do it with simplicity: he that ruleth, with diligence; he that sheweth mercy, with cheerfulness" (Romans 12:6-8).

"And God has set some in the church, first apostles, secondarily prophets, thirdly preachers, after that miracles, then gifts of healings, helps, governments, diversities of tongues" (1 Corinthians 12:28).

"And he gave some, apostles; and some,

prophets; and some, evangelists; and some, pastors and teachers: For the perfecting of the saints, for the work of the ministry for the edifying of the body of Christ" (Ephesians 4:11-12).

## Basic Principles

There are some basic principles which govern the usefulness of the charismata.

First, I believe the gifts of the Holy Spirit are for today. I know that some have interpreted 1 Corinthians 13:8 to say that prophecies have failed, knowledge has passed away, and tongues have ceased. But the arguments are tenuous at best, and I think if people were not so divided over the value (or lack of value) of speaking in tongues today, no one would attempt to drum these particular gifts out of the church.

Because I find no express statement in the Bible revoking the charismatic abilities of the Church, I must then believe that the gifts of the Holy Spirit are for today. Believing this way is comfortable because it allows me to read my Bible without discarding a thing. No supernatural event threatens a Christian who believes in the gifts of the Holy Spirit. He believes God is the same and everything which is recorded in the Bible can happen again today.

Also, it needs to be said that no one is left out in God's plan for the charismata. "The manifestation of the Spirit is given to every man to profit withal" (1 Corinthians 12:7). The word "profit" signifies development and improvement, so that too is basic to any teaching about the gifts of the Holy Spirit. They are intended to develop in our lives through use.

## Without Repentance

Yet another principle is that "the gifts and callings of God are without repentance" (Romans 11:29). God never changes His mind about the gifts imparted to us and the gifts really are permanent in our lives. This principle helps to explain why so much carnal behavior is associated with spiritual gifts. The truth is that spiritual gifts were never intended to be marks of spirituality. Gifts do not make a person spiritual any more than giving a man a hoe makes him a gardener. Only Corinthian Christianity ever assumes that spiritual gifts make people spiritual.

Having said this, it would be a serious mistake to assume that spiritual gifts are unimportant. There are some battles which will never be won in our lives apart from the charismatic manifestations. They channel power, not spirituality.

## Discovering and Receiving

The gifts of the Holy Spirit are given "severally" (1 Corinthians 12:11; 14:1), so no Christian should assume it is enough to discover his gifts. There is a lot of good teaching today about "discovering your gifts." But there may be spiritual gifts which God would be pleased to place in your life, either now or in the future.

Gifts do need to be discovered. How can

anyone "stir up" his own gift (2 Timothy 1:6) if he does not know what gift is his? At the same time, the door is open. Believers can and do receive new spiritual gifts. To ignore the scriptural commands to "covet earnestly the best gifts" and to "desire spiritual gifts" is to limit the work of the Holy Spirit.

The emphasis on discovering is often intended to be a replacement for "seeking." And seeking is many times urged when perhaps the real need is discovering. I think, as is so often the case, the truth lies in between the two.

## *Demanding Is Dangerous.*

There is, however, a very real danger in demanding spiritual gifts when God divides them "severally, as he wills" (1 Corinthians 12:11). Impudently demanding certain manifestations and dictating to almighty God obviously opens the door to the deceptive and demonic. But at the same time the Scripture says, "Covet earnestly the best gifts" (1 Corinthians 12:31). So we need to be open to the reception of spiritual gifts at all times.

But we should not presume to tell the sovereign God what He should do. In fact, of all spiritual gifts, prophecy is the only one we are told to desire especially (1 Corinthians 14:1). Interestingly enough, prophecy (or the prophetic office) is the only spiritual manifestation common to all four major lists of charismatic abilities.

## *Tongues?*

Another principle basic to the understanding of spiritual gifts is this: Not all speak in "tongues." In 1 Corinthians 12:29-30 Paul asks a series of questions: "Are all apostles? Are all prophets? Are all teachers? Are all workers of miracles? Have all the gifts of healings? Do all speak with tongues?" The answer in every case is assumed to be "no" because in the Greek the questions are preceded by the negative *me*. Some Christians speak in tongues and some do not.

To evade or avoid this statement (well illustrated in the book of Acts) is to open the door to all kinds of trouble. Making tongues a twentieth-century shibboleth has all too often unlocked Pandora's box in the church. The Scripture says, in the context of an utterance gift, to "prove all things" (1 Thessalonians 5:21).

Prophecy is to be judged (1 Corinthians 14:29). The spirits are to be tried (1 John 4:1). I am persuaded that God never intended for the Church to accept everything supernatural as divine just because it happens in the assembly.

And we who believe in the validity and worth of the gifts of the Holy Spirit today must be willing to admit that all too often tongues manifestations which have been assumed to be divine have collapsed into snarling, satanic manifestations when challenged.

## Every "Sweet Spirit" Is not Divine

Many assume every "sweet spirit" is the Holy Spirit and everything beautiful and lovely must be from God, especially when it happens in a Christian context. Nothing could be further from the truth.

When Paul exhorted his readers, he was careful not to say, "Whatsoever things are lovely, whatsoever things are true . . . think upon these things." He said instead, "Whatsoever things are true, . . . whatsoever things are lovely . . ." (Philippians 4:8). The order is truth first, beauty later. There are literally thousands of sincere Christians who have been deceived in this area.

On one occasion a missionary was appalled that I might even question that the "warm and beautiful atmosphere" in a certain assembly could be from any spirit other than the Holy Spirit. I hope the atmosphere she was describing was from the Holy Spirit. And the only reason I would question it at all is that Christians are to "prove all things." But the question does need to be raised—always.

## New Syncretism

I believe the Church has not yet learned how to deal with the dangerous syncretism which now threatens it. I have treated this subject fully in the volume referred to earlier. Historically, we have dealt with error, carnality and sin—usually in the right way. Now, however, unusual discernment is needed. We need to discern the spirits.

We need to do more than stand agape as super-spirituals make merchandise of miracles. Hawking the supernatural is as wrong as adultery any day. I see a strange paralysis among us. If a man says he has the baptism of the Holy Spirit, we forget to ask if He knows Jesus Christ as Lord. We fail to ask him if he has been born again. We fail to ask if he prays through Jesus Christ, the one mediator between God and man. We fall into the familiar error of judging a man by the supernatural which accompanies him. Instead, we ought, as Jesus said, to look for the fruit of a holy life (Matthew 7:16, 20).

There is an epidemic of spurious charismata abroad in the land. But if Satan is so concerned to imitate and deceive, we should not repudiate the genuine. Thank God for true gifts from the Holy Spirit. Thank God for thousands who experience a richer and fuller Christian life through the charismatic abilities.

With regard to the gift of speaking in an unknown tongue, it should never be a trip laid on people. No one should hustle tongues. Don't promote and don't prohibit. I am persuaded this is scriptural.

All four passages which list spiritual gifts have interesting contexts. Common to all four lists is a context relating to the body of Jesus Christ and a context relating to love. The spiritual gifts, so numerous and so diversified, make the body of Jesus Christ what it is intended to be—a functioning organism.

## *Afloat on Love*

The whole teaching is intended to float on love. At Mouila, Gabon, I shared some of this teaching with the African pastors. Beside us flowed a wide river. The spiritual gifts, I said, are like little boats. The wide river is love. When Paul says, "Follow after love, and desire spiritual gifts," he seems to be saying, "The boats are fine, just fine, but the river is what is really important!" And boats in a dry river bed are tilted and grotesque.

The spiritual gifts reflect the various parts of Christ's body. And Christ, after all, is our victory. Sometimes our Lord gives the victory through spiritual gifts.

If you have never discovered your gifts as a Christian, if you have not been open to receive new spiritual manifestations of the Holy Spirit in your life, there are some victories you have missed.

And that is reason enough to think very carefully about this chapter.

# CHAPTER 13

---

## WEAPON #12:

# SURRENDER

SOMETIMES WE COME upon things in the Christian life through a series of circumstances. This chapter, perhaps more than any other in this volume, has a history like that.

I was participating in a short-term Cree Indian Bible School at a place called Peerless Lake in the wilderness of northern Alberta. One of my assigned messages was on the subject of tithing. And as we moved through the familiar passage in Malachi 3:8-12, something new startled me. My attention was riveted on the possibility that giving the tithe allows the Lord to go to war on behalf of the tither.

The sequence is clear enough: "Bring all the tithes into the storehouse. . . . And I will rebuke the devourer for your sakes." Excitement began to mount in my own heart as these thoughts crowded into the Bible study in that log church:

Loose God's funds and you loose God's power against Satan. Could giving be a spiritual weapon? Could spiritual victories be won apart from prayer? Apart from praise? Apart from fasting? Apart from authority? Was it conceivable that spiritual victories could come through giving alone? It seemed evident to all of us there that day that there is a real sense in which tithing does exactly that. It frees the Lord to rebuke the devourer, to go to war on behalf of the tither. That has to be exciting news for Christian believers!

## *Tip of an Iceberg*

When I looked for confirmation of the principle elsewhere in the Bible, especially in the New Testament, I did not find it (though that is not to say the confirmation is not there). But I did begin to look at this "tithing power" in a new light. Perhaps it was just the tip of an iceberg. Perhaps the truth was much larger than giving. Perhaps it is obedience, I thought. Perhaps it is surrender. And that is where my thoughts led me: "surrender power." The reason tithing releases God to war against the enemy on our behalf is that in tithing we surrender our goods, or gold, to God.

When it comes to "surrender power," there is a strong, biblical case. Surrender, the epitome of weakness, allows the strength and power of almighty God to be made manifest. And the supporting Scriptures come flooding to mind.

Jacob had to surrender before he became Israel. Then God's power rested upon him as never before (Genesis 30-32).

Moses, too, was a reluctant deliverer. After God answered his objections one by one, the moment came when Moses surrendered to Jehovah (Exodus 4:29-31). Can it be coincidence that the miraculous began there? I do not think we should be surprised at this surrender power.

After the death of Moses, the commission to possess the Promised Land was given to Joshua (Joshua 1:1-9). But in 1:10 Joshua commanded the officers of the people to prepare to cross the Jordan. He surrendered to Jehovah's claims on his life. And the conquest of the Promised Land was assured by this surrender to God's power.

Gideon, too, was a great deliverer of Israel. But first he had to surrender to the call and strategy of the Almighty. He equivocated. He called for signs. But finally he obeyed the LORD fully and surrender power fell on the Midianites (Judges 6-9).

## Confrontation

In the classic confrontation between David and Goliath, the youthful David first abandoned himself to the resources of God. Saul's armor and ordinary weapons were put aside. Surrender power brought Goliath down (1 Samuel 17:31-54).

Jonah the prophet had a very difficult time surrendering to Jehovah's call. It took three days and nights in the fish's belly to convince him. But once he surrendered, revival in Nineveh was assured. Surrender power in the prophet brought the great city to its knees. The greatest revival recorded in the Bible followed. It is little wonder that Satan wars mightily against full surrender to God. He has suffered plenty in the past from God's fully surrendered servants.

After the day of Pentecost when the apostles were threatened and told to quit using the name of Jesus, they replied, "We ought to obey God rather than men" (Acts 5:29). They refused to stop preaching because they had discovered the Holy Ghost was "given to them that obey him." And they were not about to short-circuit the power. They were not about to dissipate the surrender power they had discovered.

It was a fateful day for Christendom when Saul fell to the ground blinded—when he finally cried, "Lord what wilt thou have me to do?" (Acts 9:6) Paul was mighty in deeds. He was mighty with his pen. He was destined to become one of the greatest and most influential apostles. Surrender power!

## Satan in Trouble

Paul also reminded the church at Rome of this surrender force: "For your obedience is come abroad unto all men. . . . And the God of peace shall bruise Satan under your feet shortly" (Romans 16:19-20). The only conclusion possible is that the church at Rome had obeyed Paul's earnest entreaty made earlier (Romans 12:1-2). They had presented their bodies completely to God. And that is why Satan was about to be in trouble through their obedience. It was surrender power.

A prominent contemporary Bible teacher has given a new emphasis to the yielding of rights. According to him, the yielding of personal rights unleashed the power of God to concentrate on the person in need. Here we are calling it surrender power.

The Savior exhibited it supremely. "Not as I will, but as thou wilt," He said to His Father (Matthew 26:39). His surrender to the Father was as complete as His victory over Satan was total. The prince of this world was judged and was cast out. Jesus triumphed over all the powers of hell and darkness through surrender power.

## Delightful Surrender

The delightful thing about all this is that anyone can surrender. The way to win is to lose. The way to live is to die. The way to succeed is to humble oneself.

I am still persuaded that giving the tithe sets the Lord free to rebuke the devourer for our sakes. But the reason I believe that is because it is part of a pervasive scriptural base. The surrender of money is like the surrender of anything else. It generates power.

We should leap to give all that God asks for. And we will, too, when we realize at last that full surrender to Jesus Christ is one of the mightiest blows we can ever strike at the powers of darkness. Our surrender flows ultimately to Jesus Christ.

There our surrender is united with God's power.

Then omnipotence is free to work. Do you face any impossibilities? Surrender in the name of the path that leads to victory and conquest.

## CHAPTER 14

_____

## WEAPON #13:

# SUFFERING

$O$UR SUNDAY SCHOOL class had just decided to forego its own study to listen to the cassette tape being played in a nearby classroom.

I was disgusted.

Inwardly I complained, "I came here to get something out of the Word of God and this is what they do!" But these initial thoughts I soon recognized for what they were—carnal murmurings. So I conducted a short revival service and repented, all of this within my own mind.

Then I began to read my Bible and there, to my amazement, I discovered something in the Word which I had never read before but had never really seen. Immediately I realized that it was a chapter for this book and another gentle signal from the Lord that the time had come to write.

The discovery was "suffer power."

"Forasmuch then as Christ hath suffered for us

in the flesh, *arm yourselves likewise with the same mind:* for he that hath suffered in the flesh hath ceased from sin" (1 Peter 4:1, italics mine).

Arm yourselves. The thoughts began to tumble around. Suffering for the warfare? Suffering has offensive capabilities in the Christian life? Suffering makes things happen? There were also some honest fears. It was true that Jesus' greatest power was released through His suffering, but must we all suffer? All of us want to know more about the power of His resurrection. But not so many want to know "the fellowship of his sufferings." For Paul, the two things were part of the same package; his ardent desire was "that I may know him, and the power of his resurrection, and the fellowship of his sufferings" (Philippians 3:10).

Right from his conversion Paul knew the meaning of suffering. When Ananias prayed for him, he referred to the great things Paul was to suffer (Acts 9:16). In his many journeys, the Holy Spirit's message to him was that "bonds and afflictions" awaited him (Acts 20:23).

How many of us can get excited about the great things we are to suffer? How many of us want to know about the "bonds and afflictions" which await us? And this is a related question—how many of us have a Christian experience which exudes spiritual power as Paul's did?

Suffering, so far as Paul was concerned, was part of the gospel. Suffering with Christ was a necessary antecedent to being glorified together with Him (Romans 8:17). Live a godly life and you will suffer persecution, Paul taught (2 Timothy 3:12). He also knew he was "fill[ing] up that which is behind of the afflictions of Christ in my flesh for His body's sake, which is the church" (Colossians 1:24).

Now if I can understand Paul at all, he is saying that Christians will suffer and that the result will be beneficial for Christ's body, the Church. So far as the apostle was concerned, the more his sufferings mounted up, the more the consolations were adding up too (2 Corinthians 1:4-6). Suffering produced encouragement for the church.

As I consider this concept of suffer power, I have only to look around me to realize that suffering does have a positive and powerful result.

## Surging New Power

We have had friends who are accomplished gospel musicians. They have always had an excellent ministry—so much so that we had them back twice to our conventions.

One summer, however, their son-in-law was killed just weeks before their first grandchild was to be born. Their daughter was left a young widow about to give birth. Our friends had deeply loved the young man who died. The agony of their bereavement was intense.

Later they came to sing in yet another convention. The instant they began to sing, we were all aware of surging new power in their singing. It was a tremendously moving experience to listen.

And what did we hear? We heard suffer power.

A woman who sang at our summer conventions has suffered a great deal. She has had a broken home and a broken heart. But the results of those sufferings have brought about a radiance in her life that is unusual.

And her music? She may never have released a recording of any kind. But her music exudes spiritual power. Suffer power. I know it.

Even the world sometimes senses what suffering can do. A beautiful girl, so the story goes, once had a marvelous singing voice. But something was lacking. So her singing teacher deliberately caused her to fall in love with him. Then, just as deliberately, he broke her heart. The result: superb and overwhelmingly powerful music.

## Atmosphere of Power

I had a friend who was an effective and gifted evangelist. If there is one word to describe the atmosphere when he ministered to people, and when he prayed for the sick, it was power.

The first book we ever published was his autobiography.[11] He spent nine years on a sickbed. He was slowly dying of tuberculosis. He suffered for years. Then he was miraculously healed and sent around the world to tell his story.

While his manuscript was in preparation and this chapter was surging in my heart, I realized something I had never noticed before. The key to the soul-winning evangelism that God had given him and the key to his sympathetic ministry to the sick was his former suffering. It was a ministry of suffer power.

Many of us crave Christian experiences which exude the power of God. We know God is powerful and we want Him to show His power in us. What we are less willing to do is to pass through the suffering. And one of the reasons why the sick are not always immediately healed when prayer is offered is that the time has not arrived. God may want to develop some suffer power for the consolation of His Church.

### *The Alabaster Box*

I sense, too, that there is a close relationship between suffering and brokenness. The alabaster box has to suffer, it has to be broken, before the whole house can be filled with fragrance (Mark 14:3-9). The corn of wheat has to suffer death before it can bring forth fruit (John 12:24). Real fruitfulness is often delayed because we have not been willing to suffer, because we have not been broken.

On one occasion a pastor friend had lunch with me. While we waited for the food to arrive, he took a wafer from his basket. He broke it carefully. Then he put the pieces back together. They fit perfectly.

"Is it still the same?" he asked.

"No," I said, "it is broken."

Then he said to me, "Neill, have you ever been broken?"

I had no answer. At least not then. I needed time to think.

But yes, there had been times of brokenness and suffering. In Bible college days there was a girl for whom I cared very deeply. And, yes, I suffered. But then my heart opened for the first time to the fullness of the Holy Spirit. My Christian life was radically and permanently changed. There was power which had not been there before. I know it was the power Jesus had promised (Acts 1:8). But it was something else, too—suffer power.

## Board Decision

Later, as a young pastor, a church board and a senior pastor made a decision which I found very difficult to accept. I admit there were tears. I was a brokenhearted young preacher. But God spoke to me in that hour, "Never mind. I am going to bless you anyway." And he did. In my preaching for nearly eight months afterward, until we resigned the pastorate to enter evangelism, there was a consistent and regular response Sunday after Sunday to the preaching of the Word. Conversions. Restorations. People filled with the Holy Spirit. Healings. The brokenness had unleashed power in preaching and in the ministry. Now I can see it was suffer power. I cannot help but thank God for the decision of that church board!

## Some Embarrassments

In one of my evangelistic campaigns, everything seemed to go wrong. The pastor's wife was against me and her husband sided with her. The young man who was my associate chose that campaign to tell me about a few things that were wrong with me. There were other embarrassments. (We really did have a good campaign though!) But I will honestly admit I wondered why all the buffeting was my portion.

I was not long in finding out. In the next series of meetings, a very important series, in a strategic church with a regular exposure to college students, I found more brokenness and power, more suffer power in my ministry, than I had ever known. I think the key was what I had gone through immediately before.

## Raw Gospel Power

Perhaps no concept has ever gripped me more than that of God's love. While I was writing *Revolution of Love* (Bethany House, 1972) I was held to the message of love. For two years, I could preach on nothing else. But the day the final manuscript was in the mail, I was free to preach on other subjects. But the love theme retains special affection in my heart. It is beyond doubt the most powerful thing I have ever preached. I have seen more tears, more brokenness, and more raw gospel power manifested through the love message than any other. Thank God for His love.

And will you be surprised if I tell you that coincidental with the development of that message there were satanic onslaughts and suffering? There was anxiety. Spiritual warfare on a scale I had rarely known. Satanic attacks against my ministry and my family. Attacks which were nearly ruinous.

But now I can look back. "Thank you, Lord, for the love message, and the suffering through which you worked it out."

## Alarming Turn

Now this message takes an alarming turn. If suffer power is what I am saying it is, then everyone should seek the suffering which will perfect him. Right?

Not so. That was the error of those in the history of the church who believed they had to make themselves suffer in order to achieve holiness. Long vigils of fasting—even self-inflicted wounds—were part of that mentality.

Peter, I notice, interjects an *if* into the context of suffering. "But and if ye suffer for righteousness' sake, happy are ye" (1 Peter 3:14). And he adds, "Let them . . . suffer *according to the will of God* (4:19, italics mine).

Perhaps we may conclude that when Peter urged the Hebrew Christians, "Forasmuch then as Christ hath suffered for us in the flesh, arm yourselves likewise with the same mind" (1 Peter 4:1), he was saying, "Be ready to suffer. Be willing to suffer. If it happens, you know what to expect."

## Hell Shall Not Prevail

Surely the most foolish thing Satan ever does to a church is to tear and persecute it. A tormented, suffering, bleeding church simply exudes power. Suffer power, which has perhaps lain dormant within that church for generations, suddenly springs to life. Apart from this principle the church of Jesus Christ would have perished long ago.

But it lives. The gates of hell shall not prevail against it. And its Savior shall return one day to rule because on another day long ago He suffered.

## CHAPTER 15

---

### THE SUPERWEAPON:

# LOVE

LOVE IS THE superweapon of the Christian, the weapon among all others in the Christian's arsenal which dwarfs all its competitors. And my difficulty in this chapter will be to avoid rewriting my book on love. But I will repeat some basic material and then add some things which were not in my earlier writing.

First, it needs to be stated that, in the main, two Greek words are generally used to denote love in the New Testament. *Agape* love involves personal judgment and the deliberate assent of the will. It is love in the social, or moral, sense. It is the type of love which God requires to be directed toward Himself and our Christian brethren. It is love in its "fullest conceivable form." *Phileo* love denotes friendship, fondness, and the involvement of the feelings. This love, though legitimate, is not intimate.

## Agape Love

Here we wish to discover and describe the power of *agape* love. Interestingly enough, such love is not limited to Christian believers. Unbelievers, for example, are also able to exercise it (Luke 6:32-33). Men can, in the *agape* sense, love darkness rather than light (John 3:19).

On the other hand, *agape* love in the Christian believer can get cold and stiff (Matthew 24:12). It is possible to leave one's first *agape* love (Revelation 2:4). Worst of all, *agape* love can be feigned (2 Corinthians 6:6).

Notwithstanding these negative possibilities, *agape* love is that which we are to direct to God. It is love from the will, by which we are to love God with heart, soul and strength.

If we wait to feel love toward God we may never feel it. Fortunately on the gospel train, *will* is the engine and *feeling* is the caboose. The man who expresses his love to God, even though he does not feel it, is not being dishonest. He is exercising his will. *Agape* love needs to be sought and honestly acted out; the Christian believer will then discover that this dimension of love has come alive within him.

A few years ago my wife learned this lesson, and through her learning it, I learned it too. It began when she asked a convention speaker how she could learn to love. It had taken a lot of courage for her to ask that question and the speaker's answer was so abrupt as to be almost insulting.

He said simply, "You begin by saying it." And that was all.

My wife was crestfallen and a bit rebellious. "Why should I say something I don't feel?" she thought. "Wouldn't that be dishonest?" But finally she decided since she felt God had led her to speak to that particular man, she should at least attempt to follow his advice. I am glad she did, because by following it, her life and our home were changed. Irrevocably.

## *You Do It*

Related to these statements about the human will is the scriptural teaching that love is something one does. Jesus reprimanded two Pharisees because they were leaving justice and the love of God "undone" (Luke 11:42). The implication is clear: love is something you do. It must be demonstrated in speech and deed, though not necessarily in that order.

And we certainly say that love always results in obedience. One of my friends calls this "one of the most difficult parts of the gospel." And so it is. It is comparatively easy to express love. It is inestimably more difficult to live love, to make it our life-style. But I am persuaded we must come to the place where we examine every action by the love standard. There is a profound emphasis in the New Testament on the obedience which invariably follows true love for Christ. This concept is reiterated so often (John 14:23; 14:31; 1 John 5:2, and many more references) that the only possible conclusion is that the true proof of love is obedience. Jesus said, "If a man love me, he will keep my words" (John 14:23).

Obviously, He meant it. Repetition makes it clear. You must love God. That is number one. You must love your neighbor. That is number two.

### Triple Treatment

And you must love your brother. That is the new commandment. A tremendous emphasis is given to this commandment in the New Testament if we have eyes to see it. For example, Jesus gives a threefold emphasis to several things in the New Testament: the new birth, repentance, discipleship. And this new commandment gets the triple treatment too (John 13:34; 15:12 and 15:17). When the additional biblical references to love for Christian brethren are taken into account, love for the brethren has to exceed all else in importance. If we feel uncomfortable having Christian love take precedence over the new birth, it is an unhappy commentary on our spiritual lives. Of course, only those who have been born again are able to truly love God.

Not only does our Savior command love, but He has made available the means for securing and experiencing it.

### Love Bomb

The Holy Spirit stands ready to pour love into our hearts (Romans 5:5). Love is the fruit of the

Holy Spirit (Galatians 5:22) and when a person is converted, or born again by the Spirit of God, the Holy Spirit becomes one with the human spirit. So every Christian has a love bomb within Him! It is ready to explode, and given the proper circumstances it will.

The love explosion is often called the filling or the baptism of the Holy Spirit. Call it what you may, it is available, it is within reach and all may be filled.

Paul used another figure in Colossians 3:14 where he said, "Put on charity [love]" or as you may even translate it, "Fall into love."

### Bleed Love

Surely God's love is like an ocean which we need to "fall into," be immersed in and be saturated with. When a Christian is cut, he should bleed love.

Love has its rewards too. A crown of righteousness awaits those who love His appearing (2 Timothy 4:8). There will be a crown of life for those who love Him (James 1:12). The kingdom has been promised to those who love Him (James 2:5). All things work together for good to those who love Him (Romans 8:28). God has unimaginable things prepared for those who love Him (1 Corinthians 2:9). Those who love God the most will certainly receive the most from Him.

But there are perils. Many times people are afraid to love because they feel vulnerable. What if the other person does not reciprocate?

An elderly missionary made this analogy. Loving another person is like climbing a tree and then moving out on a limb. The person can cut off the limb behind you and you will be hurt. But you must immediately climb the tree again and seek another limb. No matter how many times you fall, you must climb again. The moment you stop at the foot of the tree and refuse to climb, you have failed to love.

Love's cost is high. It cost the Father His Son. It cost the Savior His blood. But its benefits are great. Love never fails.

I am reminded of an incident which took place at one of our summer conventions. A father warned his mischievous 11-year-old boy, "If you do that again I'll punish you." He had hardly turned away before the boy had disobeyed. There was no recourse but to take the lad to a clump of trees for the punishment. The boy shuffled on ahead, rebellion showing in his shoulders and walk.

Once in the secluded area, the father took off his belt. Then he handed it to the boy. "There has to be punishment," he said, "this time you must punish me. If you don't give it to me hard, I'll give it to you after."

As the father related the incident later, he said, "I just stood there with my arms folded. I took the licking for my boy. I was weeping, and all I could say was, 'I love you, son.' "

Still the boy did not break. It was not until the

father and the son were walking back to camp that the lad finally reached up with scrawny little-boy arms and brokenly said, "I love you, too, Dad."

"My boy is still not an angel by any means," says the father today, "but praise the Lord, we turned a corner that day."

## Love Conquers All

There is not situation, no problem, no difficulty which cannot be conquered by love. It can bear all things and believe all things. It can forbear, abound, and contain. It can hold things together, it can protect, it can temper the truth without diluting it. Love is the expression of compassion. It expels fear. It exceeds speaking as a medium of expression. Love has the capacity to use supernatural gifts with supernatural effort.

Love is supreme. "Above all things have fervent charity" (1 Peter 4:8). How important is love! Love remains. "Now abideth faith, hope, charity [love], . . . but the greatest of these is charity" (1 Corinthians 13:13).

Love is really the greatest!

For years the supremacy of love was theory with me, a theology. But in recent years I have seen a few times when the love bomb has exploded among God's people. I can never be the same and I know many others can never be the same either. We were marked for eternity by God's love.

I believe in the gifts of the Holy Spirit. Some of

them are a part of my ministry and I know that the genuinely charismatic atmosphere can be tremendously powerful and fragrantly beautiful. But love is so much greater, so very much greater.

I have witnessed the explosive, expulsive power of Jesus' name. All authority is His. In such a situation the sense of God's power is very great. It almost seems sacrilegious to say love is the greatest, but it is.

I recall praying for a Cree Indian lad in the wilderness of Alberta. God was pleased to straighten his arm from an infirmity he had suffered since birth. We discovered the healing the next day when we came to church. We saw the lad shaking hands—both hands—with everybody around! In a circumstance like that, one feels a sense of awe. The miracles of God are always great.

But love is greater. Yes, it is. Yes, He is.

Because He is love.

Christ is love.

And Christ is greater than any of the things He does.

A.B. Simpson's hymn is so appropriate—

> All in all forever,
>   Jesus will I sing.
> Everything in Jesus
>   And Jesus everything.

## CHAPTER 16

---

### THE BATTLE PLAN:

# *PERSISTENCE*

*AT OUR HOUSE* my teenage son had decorated his room with all kinds of posters. Some were humorous and some had unusual messages.

One of his posters showed a cat, bedraggled and desperate, chinning himself on a pole. His whiskers and chin were still above the pole and the poster exhorted, "Hang in there, baby."

I like that. It says something about determination and persistence that needs to be said.

## Spiritual Pushovers

I notice in the kingdom of God those same qualities—persistence and determination—count a great deal. In the spiritual warfare they make the difference between conquest and defeat. You can learn all the lessons of these pages and still be a spiritual pushover. There must be a constant application of these spiritual weapons to life's problems and difficulties.

Pray—without ceasing.

Offer the sacrifice of praise—continually.

Bind and loose—repeatedly.

Fast—often.

Love—always.

Every single one of these spiritual weapons in the Christian's arsenal needs to be continually exercised and maintained.

A bit of evangelical doggerel says it, too.

> Keep on keeping on,
> Keep on keeping on,
> You'll always have the victory
> If you keep on keeping on!

And so it is.

## A Significant Encounter

Recently, I stopped for gasoline at a service station. I happened to be humming a gospel song. A young man who had also stopped there recognized the tune and said, "Are you a Christian?"

"Yes," I replied. We exchanged a few brief words and then it was time to go. But before we parted I said to the young fellow, "Hang in there!"

Afterward, I felt it had been a significant encounter. I had had an opportunity to exhort a brother to keep on going.

One of the reasons we fail in warfare, one of the reasons we do not persist, is lack of courage. We need to hear Jehovah's words to Joshua for our own ears: "Be strong and of a good courage; be not afraid, neither be thou dismayed; for the Lord thy God is with thee whithersoever thou goest" (Joshua 1:9). They would give us the courage to attack when necessary, and the will to prevail until victory comes.

## I Was Afraid

Once God was clearly telling me to do a certain thing. But I was afraid. I thought I was just being careful, but I was really a coward at heart.

Once, too, in the Scripture the prophet Samuel called upon a young man to kill Agag, a wicked king. But the youth was afraid. So the prophet took up the sword himself and he hewed Agag into pieces.

I was like that youth. For me, I knew the time had come to hew the "Agag" of my self-life into pieces. I took courage, I obeyed God, and I have no regrets. And I would like to say it again to every weary warrior on the way. Take courage because persistence pays, brothers and sisters, persistence pays.

God is the God of the breakthrough. Consistently in the Bible His character is revealed in spectacular breakthroughs. Persistence pays because God really does break through.

Jesus Christ set himself like a flint to go to Jerusalem. He went all the way to the cross. And He ever lives to make intercession for us.

So believe it. Pick up the sword and pass the Word.

And do not be surprised when things begin to happen.

# NOTES

1. Norman P. Grubb, *Rees Howells, Intercessor* (Fort Washington, Pennsylvania: Christian Literature Crusade, Paperback edition, 1973).

2. K. Neill Foster, *The Weapons of our Warfare* (Beaverlodge, Alberta: Evangelistic Enterprises Society, 1971).

3. William F. Bryan, *Tabernacle Tidings* (Toledo, Ohio: September, 1975). p.8.

4. Hal Lindsey, *The Liberation of Planet Earth* (Grand Rapids, Michigan: Zondervan Publishing House, 1974), p. 148.

5. C.I. Scofield, *The New Scofield Reference Bible* (New York, New York: Oxford University Press, 1967), p. 1215.

6. McCandlish Phillips, *The Bible, The Supernatural, and the Jews* (Minneapolis, Minnesota: Bethany Fellowship, Inc., 1970), pp. 188-199.

7. K. Neill Foster, *The Weapons of our Warfare* (Beaverlodge, Alberta: Evangelistic Enterprises

Society, 1971).

8. Some regard this passage as extra-biblical because it is not in some of the best manuscripts. However, each of the statements can be substantiated from other parts of the Scriptures, Deliverance, spiritual gifts, protection from serpents and poison, healing—teaching on all of these things can be found elsewhere in the Bible.

9. Duane T. Gish, as quoted in *Communicate* (Beaverlodge, Alberta: April, 1975) p.1.

10. K. Neill Foster, *The Third View of Tongues* (Camp Hill, PA: Horizon Books, 1994).

11. Clarence Shrier, *My God Can Do Anything!* (Beaverlodge, Alberta: Horizon House Publishers, 1975).